# SIDEKICK

## A Pregnancy Field Guide for Dudes

## BRIG BERTHOLD

*Sidekick*

## Limit of Liability/Disclaimer of Warranties

Edited by Karlee Stauffer
Cover Design by Erik Peterson
Illustrations by Tyler Carpenter
Interior Formatting by Douglas M Williams

Printed in the United States
ISBN: 978-0-9998225-1-7

# Contents

## SIDEKICK SKILLS 129

# PREFACE

The day I learned my wife was pregnant I did two things right away. First, I congratulated my wife and beamed with pride at my first measurable step toward fatherhood. Second, because I am a writer, I wasted no time starting a journal and capturing our journey the best way I knew how.

My initial motivations were simple. I wanted to remember the realities of pregnancy. Some part of me thought it would be awesome for my kids to read the funny stories and if they ever decided to start a family, maybe it would help them.

The challenges of the first trimester came at me like elephant crap hitting a jet turbine. My wife and I chose to hide the pregnancy from everyone until we reached the twelve-week mark—we will discuss this. But that decision left me with precious few resources for support and instruction. I did a bunch of online research and what I found changed my life.

Nearly everything I read or watched was negative. Men around the world were choosing to be victimized by pregnancy. A common example of this is when men say, "You're going to be ignored once there is a pregnant woman in your life," and "People will ask you how she is doing and forget all about how you are." Full disclosure, this actually happens, but why does feeling sorry for yourself have to be the response?

You are reading this book because you are now, or soon will be, living with a pregnant woman. In many ways, my time in a combat zone in Afghanistan was easier than my wife's pregnancy. Your life is way harder than it has probably ever been and that's okay.

This book is a direct response to all of the negative information I waded through. Because it began as a journal of my experiences I should make a few things clear right now.

I have made two large generalizations in the book. The first is the way I use the term "wife" to describe the pregnant woman in your life. But if this is not you, no worries. I believe in marriage and I believe that marriage is the ultimate team sport. Pregnancy is nothing if not teamwork. If you're not married, just substitute the word wife for something else, but keep reading.

Second, I assume you are going to have the baby delivered by a doctor at a hospital. I have nothing against choosing a home birth, employing a midwife or a doula. But the majority of babies are born in hospitals. If you have other plans, this book will still help you.

Regardless of your personal situation, this book is to help you see your role during pregnancy as noble. Every pregnancy is different. That means covering every possible piece of advice would lead to a book the size of "What to Expect When You're Expecting." Neither of us has time for that. Oh, and this book has pictures.

This book is a field guide. It is a reference with the simple goals of using direct language to deliver useful advice when you need it. I also think most of what happens during pregnancy is hilarious, so it's okay to laugh at your struggles. I hope you do.

# THE TEST

It was official, my life would never be the same. My wife took the pregnancy test and we saw those two blessed lines. Thanks *1st Choice* brand for being the most expensive piddle-stick we could find. We went with *1st Choice*, in part, because it was the most expensive. Our logic being, the most accurate test was likely to be the most popular, and the most expensive. We did not want to mess around with guesswork, and the *1st Choice* box claimed they had done a ton of studies, in labs, with scientists or whatever.

"Well," I said, "science is supposed to tell the truth and be accurate." Our choice was made. Our fate was sealed.

My first thought was, "Yes! I knew it." Quickly followed by, "Holy crap."

I turned to look at my wife. Her face was glowing and her eyes were dancing. She was so beautiful in that moment.

My wife and I were planning to start our family. We discussed getting pregnant at length and we put in a lot of work toward this goal. People ask me if I really knew my wife was pregnant. Yes I knew. Men know when their significant other is set to have her family reunions.

It's part of our carnal, fight-or-flight instinct. Cave men used this instinct to avoid sabre-toothed tigers. Some argue our instincts still help us avoid ferocious beasts. The only difference is, today, we only flee from danger about once per month.

What really tipped me off was the conversation I had with my wife after she was two days late. The morning we decided to buy the test, we both confessed we secretly suspected she was pregnant.

The game was on. I had officially entered the danger-zone. They may as well have gotten that annoying blonde woman from *The Hunger Games* to wish that the odds be ever in my favor.

A positive reading on that piddle stick will bring a wave of thoughts and emotions.

# List of Emotions (Comprehensive):

1. Excitement

2. Pride in your elite team of swimmers

3. Fear (more on this later)

# List of Thoughts (Not Comprehensive):

1. I hear my wife is going to change. What does that even mean?

2. Aren't babies expensive?

3. Is this a good time to go on that African Safari I planned in college?

4. When the baby comes, the first high-five will be in honor of my elite team of swimmers.

5. Do they make cool diaper bags?

6. Is our apartment/house big enough?

7. Do I make enough money?

8. If it's a little girl, should I just buy a tea set now?

9. I might as well not grow out my beard. My wife won't want it in the pictures . . . of which there will be approximately six gazillion.

10. If it's a boy, will my wife let me call him (insert comically masculine name, like Zeus)?

# WHAT MAKES A SIDEKICK?

Too many men feel they become second-class citizens during pregnancy. They are nearly forgotten as the glowing and growing woman in their life takes everyone's spotlight. Those closest to you will ask about her even when she is not present. Instead of getting upset and becoming resentful—yes, it happens—I want you to lean into your new role.

This book is intended to empower you to see your role as "number two" for what it is; a noble calling. Mindset is everything and during pregnancy, why should you *and* your wife be miserable? Pregnancy is a journey. You and your partner will grow as individuals, you'll grow as a couple, and she will literally get way bigger.

When this is all over she is the reason you get to be called daddy. A better gift is not possible.

Look, during pregnancy your wife is the hero of the story. Let's just call it what it is. Her body is ravaged by change. Her mind is assaulted by hormones. Her heart is plagued by worry and fears of new responsibility. All of that happens in just the first thirteen weeks.

Your hero is the reason you are reading this book! Okay, you helped a little. Great job, dude.

*fist bump *

Every classic hero has a sidekick, and that's you Big Guy. I should say, it can be you—but you have to earn it. You have to be worthy of the title, and that is what I am here to help you do.

When Han Solo gets in a jam, Chewbacca is there to help him through it. When Frodo Baggins starts being an overly emotional half-wit, Samwise Gamgee is ready with a pep talk. When Harry Potter starts blaming himself for the group's actions, Ron Weasley reminds Harry the decision was mutual.

As you read this book, begin to think of yourself as the trusty sidekick.

The best sidekicks bring a lot to the story. During pregnancy you will have the chance to use all of the attributes of the faithful sidekick.

1. **Bravery:** The one thing a sidekick must have is bravery. A hero's adventures are never a walk in the park, and it takes a willing volunteer to enter the unknown despite being afraid and uncertain.

2. **Comic Relief:** Heroes have a tendency to take the situation too seriously. A good sidekick knows how to help the hero smile and laugh when they need it most.

3. **Confidence:** Heroes have a rough time, and when they feel beaten sometimes they want to quit. A sidekick can reinvigorate the hero to greater action.

4. **Loyalty:** Sidekicks put the needs of the hero and the accomplishment of the mission first.

5. **Closeness:** Sidekicks take time with their hero to create a bond that withstands everything the two face.

6. **Resourcefulness:** How many times does the hero forget something or suddenly need a specific tool for the job? The sidekick remembers to bring the important tools and, if not, they always come up with something.

7. **Counterpoint:** The hero and sidekick have different skills, but their skills complement each other's.

In the end, the hero may need to be rescued. The sidekick will often be the only one in a position to help. Trust me, on the day this journey ends, as you welcome your new child into the world, your hero will need you to be there.

# MORNING SICKNESS

The second-worst part of pregnancy happens almost as soon as your wife becomes pregnant. Incidentally, the first-worst (which I like to call the most-worstest) part is the very last thing that happens.

There is almost no feasible way you've never heard of morning sickness. But I'm compelled to explain because some of you may not be familiar with the phenomenon.

Morning sickness is the first sign that your wife's body is trying to kill her. We call this pregnancy. Her hormones realize one of your swimmers made a new friend. I'm not entirely convinced the chemical response isn't an evolutionary response to an ancient man-hater tendency, but I digress. Here's what you need to know about, other than tacos, to get through morning sickness.

In almost all cases I could find, the nausea, vomiting, and overall hung-over feeling won't start until the fourth week of pregnancy. This is also the earliest point of detection with a home pregnancy test.

Why it happens is not important. What is important is how to deal with it. Mild morning sickness can be managed by eating regularly— like every 90 mins. I have never met a pregnant woman who didn't already do this.

For more severe cases, regularly eating or drinking ginger, bland crackers and bread, or even a hot pad across the woman's hips can ease the pain. There are rumors about a vitamin cocktail which may be safe for women facing more intense morning sickness. Unfortunately, excessive vomiting can quickly lead to dehydration. This can put your wife's health at risk. If your wife cannot keep fluids down and is vomiting too much, you need to see a doctor immediately.

The sidekick can do three things:

1. **Supplies:** Always have a cracker and a lightly carbonated ginger ale with you. Also, have a stockpile at home. This will

help you avoid the need to leave your hero at midnight when she needs you with her.

2. **Love and Kindness:** With her out, you need to pick up the slack. Welcome to pregnancy. You should expect to do a lot of the housework while your wife works through this phase. It's okay. You can do it.

3. **Patience:** Remember, your wife has never been through this before. She is scared and in pain, and she needs you to be as understanding as possible. She is going to say crazy things, ask for crazy things, and probably do crazy things. Have patience.

## Brewing Herbal Tea

Unless you're already a tea brewing magician, you will want to avoid loose-leaf tea in a strainer. Just buy pre-made tea bags. The key here is flavor and speed.

1. Bring a pot or kettle of water until it's wicked hot (205 degrees Fahrenheit). If you get really desperate you can heat a mug of water in the microwave but it's not optimal.

2. Make sure you have a clean mug

3. When the hot water is ready, place the tea bag in the hot water. (Tea in hot water is called "steeping")

4. Most herbal tea should be steeped in 205 degree water for approximately 4 minutes. If you leave it in much longer than that, the tea will become bitter.

# Brewing Herbal Tea

# Prenatal Vitamins

What your hero eats will probably not contain all the necessary nutrients. Because most of us suck at food, vitamins are the only way to guarantee the baby is getting what it needs.

Prenatal vitamins are designed to make up for these deficiencies, but they are not all created equal. Our doctor suggested my wife take additional supplements to improve any deficiencies in her prenatal vitamins.

Vitamin D: 2,000 international units (IU) per day. There is some debate but, it is suggested that vitamin D helps regulate your wife's calcium and phosphorus. This is important because you want your kid to have strong bones and healthy teeth.

Folic Acid (vitamin B9): One milligram. Research shows your wife needs 600 to 800 micrograms (mcg), or 0.6 to 0.8 milligrams (mg) per day. For me, it's easier to remember at least one mg each day. Folic acid is the primary defense against spina bifida. The birth defect means your child's spine is improperly formed. At its worst, the child is born with its spinal cord and all of its protective coverings out of position.

Calcium Citrate: 1,200-1,400 mg. One side effect of taking calcium supplements is the development of kidney stones. If your wife chooses to take calcium supplements—because she is lactose intolerant for instance—she needs to be extra hydrated to help prevent this.

Omega 3: These fatty acids are critical for the development of your baby. There are two things to remember when you look into Omega 3 supplements for your wife's pregnancy:

1.  It must be plant based. Fish oils may contain mercury, which can actually harm the child.

2. DHA is the key ingredient to search for. Your wife needs a recommended 300 mg of DHA during pregnancy and while breastfeeding. Make sure she can get that much each day within the Omega 3 pills.

Your hero has to take her vitamins. It's as simple as that. Your job is to remind her and, if she's resistant, to hide them in her tacos.

# NAUSEA AND YOU: A DRIVING LESSON

Whether you drive a BMW or a minivan, pregnancy is not the time for breaking land-speed records. My wife would rather I drive by default, but nausea makes her care less about being the driver. Since she is white-knuckling her way through nausea, I'm extra careful about how I drive.

Driving is a necessity for most people. Your wife knows this, but she would rather get fired than get into the car to go anywhere during the first trimester. There is a way to enjoy this, barely. You get to practice driving like a grandpa. You'll learn how to go the speed limit. You'll take right hand turns at three miles per hour. You'll stop at least three car lengths away from anything. This is all to avoid cleaning up the chunks your wife just blew on the dash, or in your lap, or in the backseat because she missed the window.

In the first trimester, all you can do is be as careful as possible. Frantic driving, of any kind, will devastate your wife. The rest of your driving lessons will come during the third trimester. In the third her belly will feel, to her, like a large bowl of soup. Everything you do in the car will feel like a sloshing crock pot filled with chili she is trying to avoid spilling.

# HOW TO PULL A CAR OVER FOR VOMIT

# Food, Vomit, Food!

Let me tell you a story. First, your wife gets hungry. This happens as abruptly and as frequently as you think about sex. Then—if you're lucky—your wife announces what she is craving. If you're unlucky, she announces that she needs something salty "or" sweet. Your life is extra hard when she is hungry, but also unsure of what she wants.

See, your wife will get nauseated when she is hungry. So you, being the faithful sidekick, fetch her some crackers, a hamburger, or a side of beef. She eats some (not all) of the food, and you think the crisis has been averted. The wave of sickness passes, her stomach calms down, and she keeps eating. Literally the next moment she will realize she has eaten too much. Even if she doesn't say so, you will know when this happens. She will throw her food and begin hunting for the nearest vomit receptacle.

Sometimes, she pukes. Sometimes, she doesn't. Without fail, she will return from Vomit Castle without an appetite. This will only last a short time. The next thing you know, she has both hands pressed to her face expressing how hungry she is. Groundhog day becomes groundhog hour.

As her sidekick, you have a few options:

1. Be prepared with a small snack. At all times have something salty, something sweet, and something sour. Examples include: club crackers, a small sucker, and lemonheads. Always get the smallest version possible. Don't get a tootsie-pop, get a dum-dum. Have these in your glove box, your briefcase, etc., and be ready.

2. Part of the vomit issue could be traceable to heartburn or acid reflux. Encourage your wife to have some antacid chews in her bag or purse. She will probably eat them like a stoner with the munchies, so you should carry some too.

3. Find a cracker or type of bread that doesn't upset her stomach. Keep some by her side of the bed. Sleeping will represent the greatest amount of time she will go without eating. Because pizza delivery is slow in the middle of the night you will end up running for tacos if she wakes up hungry.

* *Being at work for as long as possible is not an option.*

# Cooking, Part 1

# Cooking, Part 2

## Cooking For Your Wife

**Pro tip**: Do not screw this up by thinking you can cook for your wife.
**Pro tip**: Hot sauce is key. / Don't discount hot sauce.

**Step 1**: Ask your wife what kind of tacos she wants.

**Step 2**: Ask her how many tacos she wants.

**Step 3**: Get in your car and drive to the nearest taco joint. Bonus points: Drive to her favorite taco joint.

**Step 4**: DO NOT get a different kind of taco than your wife asked for.

**Step 5**: ALWAYS get more tacos than your wife asked for.

**Step 6**: Deliver tacos to your wife.

**Step 7**: Do all of this as quickly as possible.

# BLOODHOUNDS
# AND BAKING SODA

Before pregnancy, your wife may not have been able to smell much. That is all about to change. Soon her nose will start picking up smells like never before. Some of those odors will be real and some will be imagined. Either way, she's going to end up with a super sonic nose.

Cleaning will take on new a meaning. You think you live in a clean home? You're probably wrong. Trust me, dirt, dust, and everything else will magically begin to offend your wife.

Your first thought will be to pick up a rag, get it wet, and start wiping things down. Only attempt this if you can do so with a certified clean rag. Something you just pulled the tag off is preferred.

Sterilizing wipes, like Lysol wipes, are a great idea if you want to add vomit to your cleaning list. Only use wipes if you can clean with the windows open and wait one hour before your wife enters the room. Bathrooms are more difficult, as they need more time to burn off the new "clean smells."

You should know, there is no such thing as a "clean smell." Air fresheners, candles, and Febreze don't actually smell clean. They fill the air with powerful smells designed to distract your nose from the nasty you live in. All of these products will make things worse for your wife.

Carpet is one of the major odor criminals in your home. When it comes to carpet, you have a few options. Hire a cleaning service is the most expensive option, but it is the best way to clean carpet. The cheapest option is baking soda. This simple product is great! Remember when you were a kid, there was always a small open box of baking soda in your refrigerator? That white powder is an odor conquistador.

## Baking Soda Deodorizer Guide

**Step 1**: Vacuum your carpet like you've never vacuumed before. Empty the bag/canister before you start. Go slowly, be super thorough. Move stuff out of the way if you can and vacuum under everything. This step picks up all of the surface level dirt.

**Step 2**: Dump baking soda on the carpet. It will come out, don't worry. No, it won't stain or bleach your carpet. Be liberal and cover the entire carpeted area. Don't forget about stairs and carpet near bathrooms and eating areas.

**Step 3**: Walk away. You will want to let the soda sit on your carpet for several hours while the soda does it's thing.

**Step 4**: Vacuum again. Obviously you'll need to clean the soda from your carpet. Baking soda traps odor. By vacuuming the soda, you also remove the odor. Again, be thorough and go slow.

# Baking Soda Deodorizer Guide

# BODY ODOR

As your wife's canine sense of smell develops into superhuman, her nose will send odd signals to her brain. In the first trimester you're no longer the masculine sex symbol you were yesterday. Now you're a stinky hobo who can't spell shower to save your life. She will smell you, herself, and anyone else within the same zip code.

We all sweat at night, even if we didn't have sex. Before your hero got pregnant, either she didn't notice the smell, or it never bothered her. All of that has changed in the first trimester. Your natural smells aren't the only thing that will set her off either. Here are some down and dirty steps to help her avoid hating everything:

1. Buy the most boring, odorless soap and shampoo you can find.

2. Try to get out of bed before your wife does. If you can wake up first, that's even better. This way you will be less likely to offend her. You will also escape the inevitable grumbling and possible gagging noises.

3. Brush your teeth! Basically, do this as often as you can without making your gums bleed. This step is especially important first thing in the morning. Since you're springing out of bed anyway, you might as well go brush those teeth. Floss is also highly recommended, but I'm no dentist.

4. If you, and your wife, love a certain cologne, you should put it away. Hide the bottle until at least the third trimester. If you would rather be safe, wait until you have a baby in your life to break it out. Your wife will learn to hate anything that makes her gag in the first trimester. Since most everything makes her gag you don't want to run the risk.

# Your First OB Visit

Your first visit at the OBGYN can be a lot to handle. Many doctors will not even see a newly pregnant woman until she reaches the eight week mark.

In preparation for the appointment, have your wife drink a ton of water. Don't let her go to the bathroom before the appointment, she will need it. I recommend going with your wife to the visit so you can hold her hand, her purse, and anything else she nervously thrusts your direction.

Plan to spend at least an hour and a half at the doctor's office. Your doctor will order an ultrasound. This helps him or her check to see if everything is going well on the insides. During this visit you will not hear the heartbeat.

Be prepared for your baby to look super weird during that first ultrasound. Not all men feel this way, but I did.

The doctor or nurses may tell you this, but it's normal for your wife to see some spotting (bleeding) after the first exam. However, encourage your wife to listen to her body and if she thinks something is wrong—it doesn't matter what the doctor said—get it checked.

Miscarriage will likely be a topic of conversation. Our doctor shocked us with statistics, so I'm going to list them now to prepare you for when the time comes. You may, or may not, want to share this with your wife.

- All pregnancies have a 24% chance of failure in the first 13 weeks.

- Once the heartbeat is positively identified, the chance of failure drops to 5%.

- By the 13-week mark, the risk of failed pregnancy drops to less than 1%.

Many women miscarry during their first pregnancy. The majority of miscarriages occur in the first seven weeks of pregnancy. However, an estimated 15%-20% of all pregnancies in the US fail before 20 weeks. For more information about miscarriage, see the next chapter.

# MISCARRIAGE

This is not an easy topic to discuss, but it will be relevant for many first-time fathers.

Miscarriage happens when a woman's body spontaneously aborts a pregnancy. In the United States, failed pregnancies are classified as miscarriages up to the 20th week.

Miscarriages in the first trimester are mainly caused by a fetal imbalance of chromosomes; either too many or too few. When this happens the woman's body naturally aborts the fetus. There is a ton of speculation as to why this occurs. I am not diminishing the challenge of miscarriage, but most of the available information seeks to ease emotional burdens rather than providing scientific justification.

Of course many other factors can lead to miscarriage and precious few can be intentionally influenced. Here are a few things your hero may be able to control:

1. Too much or too little body weight can increase chances of miscarriage.

2. Caffeine intake, even in seemingly moderate quantities, increases the risk of miscarriage. Give up caffeine as soon as you suspect your partner may be pregnant.

3. Taking antidepressant medication during pregnancy has been proven to increase a woman's risk of miscarriage. That being said, a woman currently taking antidepressants who becomes pregnant does not necessarily need to stop taking therapeutic medication. She should not simply stop. Rather, the woman must consult her physician as soon as possible.

4. It should go without saying that alcohol, tobacco, and drugs place a fetus in serious jeopardy. These substances dramatically increase the chance of a failed pregnancy.

Miscarriage is a disappointment at best. More often, it can be devastating. A woman may experience feelings of guilt, failure, and subsequent self-blame. These thoughts and feelings can quickly lead to depression without a resilient attitude and care from those closest to her. Unfortunately, substance abuse is becoming more and more common in the wake of this tragedy.

All men deal with miscarriage differently. Some men never experience feelings of loss. Other men will confront emotional challenges as deeply as their wife does. Remember, it is okay to acknowledge your feelings for what they are. Seek help if you need it. Being strong for your wife is challenging but it can be even harder if you are not also being taken care of.

Miscarriage can be just as devastating to an expectant father as the mother. Depression is not something to be taken lightly. If you or your wife find yourself in this situation, I recommend the following:

1.  Have a culture of open and honest communication between you and your hero. She needs to feel safe coming to you with her concerns. Her fears must be received with empathy, love and unfailing support.

2.  Do all you can to help her understand the failed pregnancy is not her fault. At the same time, do not diminish her feelings. She will be heartbroken and you need to remember she is allowed to be heartbroken. Trying to convince her those feelings are baseless may lead to closed-off communication. Listen to her. Validate her feelings. But help her remember it's not her fault.

3.  You need someone you can talk to. Someone other than your wife. I'm not suggesting you should not share your feelings with your wife. You absolutely should. What I'm saying is, you need to have someone who is removed from the situation who can be there for you. Look for someone who will be careful with your feelings like your dad, your mom, a best friend, or a close relative.

4.  If you, or your wife, are having thoughts or feelings of hurting yourself or others you need to seek medical help immediately.

# Cleaning a Toilet

## Cleaning The Toilet

**Pro tip**: The Works is the only toilet cleaner worth a Damn.

**Tools**:
- Clorox wipes
- The Works
- Toilet bowl brush

**Step 1**: Squeeze the works inside the toilet bowl. Specifically target the upper lip inside the bowl. Let the cleaner sit while you complete steps 2 & 3.

**Step 2**: Scrub the outside of the toilet with Clorox wipes. Don't forget the outside of the bowl.

**Step 3**: clean the floor around the toilet bowl. All the way around.

**Step 4**: Scrub inside the toilet bowl with brush. Clean all surfaces, even if they are white. Hit the inside lip of the bowl pretty hard.

**Step 5**: Flush the toilet.

# DECIDING TO ANNOUNCE

One of the main questions you will be asking yourself is, "When do we tell people?" Many people have answered this question. I have sifted through all of that and came up with two reasonable answers.

The first option is to announce a pregnancy whenever you want. The basic argument being that the prospect of a new member of the family will bring joy to those you tell. You could ask yourself if you and your wife are comfortable going public. If you are comfortable, go ahead and spread the joy.

The second option is to wait until the pregnancy reaches the magical 13-week mark. By 13 weeks you will have reached the end of the first trimester. As the chances of miscarriage are higher in the first trimester, many couples choose to wait before spreading the joy.

Everyone's initial decision is different. I say that because we wanted to wait. However, a few people in our lives needed to know well before 13 weeks. My wife was sick constantly. Nausea was ever-present. Frantic sprints to the bathroom were common. Her sense of smell would have put bomb dogs to shame. Her appetite was insatiable.

We decided to tell our parents and her supervisors at work. If she was acting odd at home, you can bet she was acting strange at work. Luckily, my wife worked with a wonderful group of people. They were caring and understanding even though she was late regularly.

The decision to tell our parents was simple. We needed help. Neither of us had ever faced pregnancy before. Pregnancy can be a very genetic thing, and your wife needs to be able to ask people for advice. Your job is to let her.

You may be worried about things getting around too far. I know you don't want to have to explain a miscarriage to everyone and their dog. But, if this is your wife's first pregnancy, she needs support from other people. As her sidekick, you should help her feel comfortable with communicating with anyone she needs to.

**Great Sidekick Move:** Help her know it's okay for her to ask for help. Do this before she brings it up and you'll be winning. Aggressively support her feelings.

# How to Announce

If this is your first pregnancy, you probably have no idea that people announce pregnancies. It's a lot like a wedding announcement. Here is what you need to know:

1. Don't do anything cheesy or embarrassing. Stay classy. When in doubt, go traditional.

2. If your wife already knows what she wants, let her do it. Buy the tiny moccasins, make the custom t-shirts, and take a picture. Only protest if you're prepared for her to decide she might want a new sidekick.

3. Grandmas and Grandpas don't know what the internet is. Stop being stingy with the postage and send some actual announcements. Most other people can get an email.

4. Only BuzzFeed and Pinterest care about your artistic ability. Everyone else just wants to celebrate with you. Don't stress over quality.

# PREGNANCY AND FITNESS

A lot of questions arise when it comes to working out during pregnancy. There are a few best practices out there, but everything else is rumor or myth.

I'm including this topic in the first trimester so you can get a head start.

Regardless of your wife's level of fitness before pregnancy, any activity is always better than a completely sedentary lifestyle. All physical activity should only be conducted after consulting your wife's doctor. Other than that, she just needs to be self-aware and as active as possible. For most women, fitness during pregnancy is encouraged and no, it won't hurt the baby.

Generally, women do not want to workout during the first trimester. Depending on the severity of their morning sickness, they may not even be able to get out of bed. If your hero can workout during the first trimester without introducing her last meal to the entire gym, you should encourage her to workout. For everyone else, wait until the morning sickness passes.

The second trimester is the best time for fitness. Something about greater blood-flow makes most pregnant women able to workout better than ever. My wife went to a CrossFit class every day until midway through the third trimester.

When it comes to fitness during the third trimester, every woman is different. Some women are just too oddly-shaped and imbalanced for anything more coordinated than reaching for a box of Thin Mints. Other women are superhuman. One of my wife's friends did a CrossFit workout in the morning and casually lunge-walked the 20 miles to the hospital that afternoon to deliver her baby. I think she was doing an incline press during labor, but I wasn't there.

There are two general rules to go by: First, if your wife already has a fitness lifestyle, she needs to do what she can to keep it up. Modify as needed and be self-aware. Second, if fitness is not part of your wife's lifestyle, she needs to be careful but encourage her to be more active. Fitness during pregnancy lowers a woman's chances of developing gestational diabetes and helps to avoid the need for unplanned cesarean sections (C-section).

You would be surprised what walking can do for a woman's health. Another common activity during pregnancy is aquatic fitness. In either activity your wife develops her cardiovascular and core strength.

# FITNESS FOR FUTURE DADS

Having a new baby in your life is a lot like being forced to haul a 10 pound dumbbell around. But, unlike dumbbells, your baby will continue getting larger and heavier. Not only are kids heavy, they also require a ton of baggage wherever they go—which they refuse to carry.

For these reasons, I strongly encourage all soon-to-be fathers to hit the gym. Better swole than sorry, in this case. Lucky for you, I have a few suggestions to make the getting started easier.

1. You have to do resistance training. Whether you lift weight and follow a program, do bodyweight (calisthenic) work, or join a class—like CrossFit—you should begin right away.

2. Cardio is good, but it won't help you lug an increasingly heavy car seat around. Spending less time on the treadmill is good for you anyway.

3. For those of you not previously following a program, don't worry. Most really decent plans have a 12-week progression. This is not an excuse to wait until the third trimester to begin. Instead, complete three programs while you wait for baby to show up and reap the rewards.

4. Aside from physical benefits, fitness will give you time away from home and away from work. Add some tunes and let any pent up tension flow from your secret angry place.

## Muscles Critical to Fatherhood

1. **Front Deltoid**: This is your shoulder, and you'll work it constantly.
2. **Biceps**: Think about all the times you'll hold the kid in the crook of your arm.
3. **Abs**: You are going to use your core more than ever.
4. **Quads**: Because you don't want to throw out your back lifting all that baby gear. Lift with your legs.

# Muscles Critical to Future Fatherhood

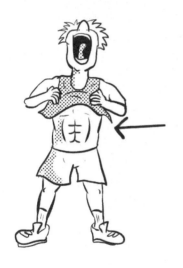

# DIAPERS

Gentlemen, buy diapers. I am putting this in the first trimester because I know you will ignore my advice the first time. The average newborn soils themselves 10 to 15 times per day. Variance is due primarily to formula-fed versus breast-fed diets. At the time of this writing, it is widely estimated that you will use around 320 diapers just in the first month of baby's life.

That number drops slightly to between 8-10 changes per day for the rest of the first year. This means you can expect to burn through approximately 240 diapers per month from months 1-12. Begin a stockpile as soon as possible. Stocking up on diapers will give you the peace of mind you won't be able to buy when baby arrives. Your newly impoverished and sleep deprived self will thank you.

Planning to obtain the correct amount of diapers in the appropriate sizes will give you anxiety attacks. Since every child grows differently, and since you want to prepare, here is the conventional wisdom:

**N or NB:** Newborn is almost always the least used diaper size. Kids seem to grow out of them quickly.

**Size 1:** 1,000

**Size 2:** 500

**Size 3:** 1,000

**Size 4:** 1,000

**Size 5:** 1,000

You will also need a metric ton of baby wipes. Luckily, wipes are "one-size-fits-all." Rock star diaper changers may be able to do a normal diaper with one wipe. However, mere mortals can expect to start at three to four wipes per change. That's at least 30 wipes per day for the first month. Once changing slows a bit, if you still use three per change, you will only use between 20 and 30 per day for the first year.

Not all diapers are created equal. Some won't fit right. Others may cause rashes and skin irritation. The best thing to do is to buy hypo-allergenic diapers if you want a stockpile. Otherwise, buy from a place that will allow you to return one brand for another if baby doesn't like the one you bought.

# ADJUSTED EATING HABITS

Food is one of the funniest things about pregnancy. Your wife will crave the oddest things at the strangest moments. Being the good sidekick you are, you will eagerly supply her every wish. After she has what she asked for, it probably won't taste good. This will happen.

Not everything tastes the way it should. My sister-in-law hilariously described mint ice cream as tasting like mustard.

Other than warn you—and tell you it will be okay—here are a few tips:

1. If she can't eat or drink something, it will help if you don't eat or drink those things either. At least, don't do it in front of her. Things she will need to avoid are:

   - Sushi and most fish
   - Caffeine
   - Smoking
   - Alcohol
   - Drugs (including most medication)
   - Cured meats (salami & bacon)

2. Know the nearest taco joints to your house and anywhere else you may find yourself.
3. Buy a jar of un-cut pickles. Dill seems to be better than sweet for most women.
4. Keep orange juice in the house because she will crave the citric acid.

Everything else is unpredictable. Most of the time, cravings represent some deficiency in your wife's nutrition. If she is craving brownies, however, it doesn't mean she is not getting enough brownies. My wife wanted things other women would have hated, other than tacos, which seems to be the universal pregnancy craving.

# List of Foods to Avoid

**List of Foods to Avoid**

- Sushi and Most Fish
- Caffeine
- Smoking
- Alcohol
- Drugs (including most medication)
- Cured Meats (Salami & Bacon)

# PREGNANCY BRAIN
## AND THE YIN-YANG

We need to talk about pregnancy brain. If it hasn't begun already, your wife's brain will start turning to mush. She is quite busy thinking about important things like ice cream, pickles, and sleep. Everything else is less important, despite what you think.

If your wife is the hero, and you are her sidekick, pregnancy brain is the villain.

Pregnancy brain leaves logic and memory standing in the welfare line, patiently waiting for the odd manual labor job. That's a best case scenario. At its worst, anarchy brings a coup d'etat in your wife's brain and emotion now reigns supreme.

Prepare for shifting priorities, adjusted expectations, and increased workload. Your wife will go full Yin—you have to go Yang . . . hard.

# Guy's Night

D on't forget to take care of yourself. You need to have guy's night so you don't go crazy.

Guy's night during pregnancy is going to be different. The first thing to keep in mind is that you're still on duty. The second thing to keep in mind is that after guy's night, you're on duty.

Everyone knows the first rule of guy's night. You don't talk about guy's night. *fist bump* While you are a full-time sidekick, there are a few more rules I suggest you follow:

1. **Don't get arrested:** If you do something stupid and you get arrested, you may not be available when your wife needs you. It will likely require her to take care of you. Guys, that's not what we're doing here.

2. **Don't get hurt:** If you hurt yourself because you accepted a bet that required you to jump off of (or over) anything, into anything, at any speed, you will not be able to be the sidekick your wife needs.

3. **Don't get drunk:** If you get drunk you cannot run to the store for emergency resupply of ginger ale and crackers. You also don't want to be so hungover the next day you become grumpy and irritable. That's not going to help anyone.

The best way to handle guy's night is to encourage your wife to schedule girl's night at the same time. Just like you, she will want time away and a change of scenery. If you plan to be apart at the same time, you can rest assured she will be taken care of by her friends. This increases your ability to relax and enjoy yourself. Also, she'll call less.

# Language
# and Other Lifestyle Changes

In the movies, pregnant women are always scolding the husband to stop cursing. This phenomenon is real. If cursing is not a part of your life, expect any rough language or angry outburst to be treated the same way. After much thought, open conversation, and my fair share of scolding, I have come up with some ideas as to why this happens.

A pregnant woman's hormones are constantly in flux. The standard result is an increase in her sensitivities. Temperatures, sunlight, and aggression are just a few examples.

Because you are the best sidekick a hero could ask for, you will try to ease up on some things. Here are a few suggestions of things you may want to change before a stern scolding comes flying your way:

1.  Limit or cut cursing.

2.  Avoid road rage.

3.  Don't watch movies with lots of violence.

4.  Limit or cut out any angry or aggressive music. Also, mellow music with suggestive language is to be avoided.

5.  If you're going to have guy's night, and you should, do it away from your home.

These changes may present a serious challenge for some men. By following these general guidelines your wife will be happier, your home will feel more welcoming, and you won't get in as much trouble.

Give it your best effort and any change you can make will put a smile on her face.

# 3 LIBIDO — 2 LIBIDO — 1 LIBIDO — NONE!

A woman's sex drive has been a mystery to men since the first time Eve only wanted a back rub. This fact does not change during the first trimester. In fact, things get even more challenging.

For those who were actively trying to get pregnant, you were probably having more sex than ever. You were rolling in carnal, animalistic bliss, and it was your wife's idea. Transition that life into a nearly barren, solo, existence. An occasional oasis may present itself as you sleep.

Those who weren't tracking ovulation cycles will still begin a life of sexual solitude. Legend has it, some women do not refuse sexual advances during the first trimester. If your wife fits this category, count your blessings.

One thing is universal, a woman on the verge of vomiting does not feel particularly horny. She doesn't feel sexy. She feels disgusting both inside and out. Your experience will not be the same as anyone else's, but a libido drop is not the end of the world.

1) Tell your own libido to send you postcards from dreamland for a while. It's going to be okay.

2) Talk about sex with your wife. Agree on how you will handle sex during the first trimester. After that conversation, expect less sex than you agreed to.

## Three Types of Days

My experience has shown that I had three types of days during the first trimester:

1. Days when I forgot my wife was pregnant

2. Days when fear of the unknown prevailed

**3.** Days when I was filled with excitement

Not everyone will experience days where they forget their wife is pregnant. Especially if their wife is always sick or they're constantly helping to satisfy her odd food cravings. But, on days when you are pretty busy, or your wife is handling things well, you may forget. I did.

Everyone will experience days when fear is clearly in the lead. You'll be afraid of not making enough money, or of being a student while trying to be a husband and a father. These feelings are normal— you would be crazy if you never had them.

The best days are filled with fun thoughts of Nerf gun battles, tea parties, Lego building, movie nights, school science projects, and more. At this stage of your baby's development, your excitement grows, even if the kid's progress is behind the scenes.

# INTRODUCTION
## TO PHASE TWO

Once the first trimester winds down you will notice a calm settling into your life. Most women no longer deal with the symptoms of nausea and extreme fatigue in the second trimester. Consider this the reward of a well-earned victory over the absurdity of phase one.

I called my mom about two weeks into the second phase of pregnancy. I told her the pregnancy had become boring and that I kept forgetting my wife was pregnant. A part of me worried that I was a cold-hearted jerk. As though forgetting about the looming event were even possible, honestly, it happened.

My mom assured me I was normal, and she gave me the best definition for the second trimester—"the sweet spot." Looking back, she could not have been more correct.

In phase two, life is good. Everyone knows you're expecting and they are as happy about it as you are. Your hero will start to really show her bump, she'll begin buying fun maternity clothing with creative openings, and you get to geek out about baby gear.

The late-night Taco Bell cravings will fade as your wife's hormones may bring about new cravings, the kind you probably won't want to run away from. Life takes on a shade of normalcy while you happily await the arrival of your new baby.

However, the second trimester isn't all sunshine and rainbows. Don't forget you have a job to do. When Bruce Wayne is at a charity event, tipping his hat and toasting his friends, Alfred is analyzing security tapes and keeping an eye on the headlines. Phase two is your chance to gather the tools you need to get your hero through the third trimester and to prepare for the new kid.

In this section, we'll go over what you can expect and some keys to successful phase three planning.

# Master
# the Double-Check

Pregnancy brain, as we have said, is very real. For this reason, it is in your best interest to double-check some things for your wife. You already know that all of the remembering is your job. In this context, your hero truly doesn't realize she left the cupboards open. Likewise, if your refrigerator doesn't beep at you after it's been open too long, you'll want to check that too.

It is not your wife's fault and getting upset with her will definitely cripple your sidekick efforts. Rather than get angry, just do a "once around the world." Before you leave the house, take five seconds and turn off every light in the house. After a meal, casually stroll into the kitchen to put away the milk and other perishables.

If your subtle checks make your wife angry, or if they hurt her feelings, there are two ways to handle it.

1.  You could ignore her obvious feelings. This is the wrong idea.

2.  You can communicate.

A calm, gentle, and loving explanation about how you are trying to help will win you points. She needs—and wants—you to show her you are looking out for her. Remind her that you want to make her life as comfortable as you can.

In most cases, you won't need to say anything. She will notice you being good to her and that's the point. Genuinely serve her by checking the laundry, tidying the kitchen, and putting gas in the car. The only thing left to do is know that you are a great sidekick!

# Maternity Clothes

Most women begin to show during the second trimester. This means your hero's belly will begin to grow. She is not getting fat and any suggestion about her weight from you—or anyone else—will end in disaster.

Her increasing size will require a new wardrobe. If you live near your hero's family, or some of her close friends, the clothing situation could be taken care of without your help. You supply the money and the women will handle the rest.

On the other hand, you may end up in a shopping situation. If you do, here's what you need to know:

1. Most maternity clothing is slightly more expensive than you may be used to. In my experience, prices aren't disgusting, but doing a complete wardrobe overhaul in one shopping trip could easily break the bank.

2. When your hero tries something on, she may ask you a variation of the question "does this look okay?" Your best bet is to use what I call the comfort comment.
   Example: "That looks really comfy, babe."
   If this is her first pregnancy, she is not—at this point—worried only about comfort. The comfort comment helps her to consider more than fashion.
   If she presses you for more, a safe answer is "I like it," always coupled with a casual shrug. You will either help her feel good about the item of clothing, or she will stop asking you. Your goal is not to get out of evaluating her department store fashion show. Your goal is to help her be physically and mentally comfortable.

3.  If something looks uncomfortable, or if she is not sure whether something will be comfortable, help her ditch the item. Just say, "That looks a bit uncomfortable. What do you think?"

4.  Go to a maternity clothing store without your hero one time. Ask questions, get help understanding what pregnant women like and don't like, and then buy your wife something that will definitely be comfortable, like a sweater. Choose something without a pattern, in a neutral color, and "cute"—which you should confirm with another woman at the store.

Finally, let's talk about bottoms. Neither you nor your hero wants to spend the next six months in sweatpants. Okay, she may want to, but it's not a good idea. These days, they make awesome pants for pregnant women with a built-in elastic band around the waistline. You can find all types of pants from jeans to dress pants with this feature. This way she can be comfortable and look nice.

# PREGNANCY AND SLEEP

Science tells us that a typical woman needs more sleep in a twenty-four-hour period than a typical man. You think you know now, but you have no idea. My decidedly unscientific opinion is that a pregnant woman would sleep between fifteen and eighteen hours per day if she could. She would only wake long enough to relieve herself, eat a taco, and call her mother before going back to sleep.

This utopian dream is only possible before the first child arrives. As her faithful sidekick, you have two jobs here.

1. Help your wife sleep well at night and let her take a nap during the day if it's possible.

2. Make sure your wife isn't getting too much sleep. That is the hard part. I hate to tell you this, but nobody is sure what "too much sleep" is. The only tool I can give you is to watch closely to make sure she isn't getting lethargic.

During the second trimester, some of her hormones balance out and her body isn't freaking out as much. The stress and excitement from the first trimester have passed and the routine of the second trimester will calm her. And, if you add in a healthy amount of activity—even physical fitness—these factors will combine to help her sleep the best she can. You would be amazed by how much mental health can impact a person's sleep. Physical activity will dramatically help your hero's mental health, and by default, her sleep will be improved.

There are a few things you should be on the lookout for. While leg cramps, heartburn, and extra-vivid dreams are normal, if any of these symptoms get out of control your hero needs to see her doctor.

# Foot Massage

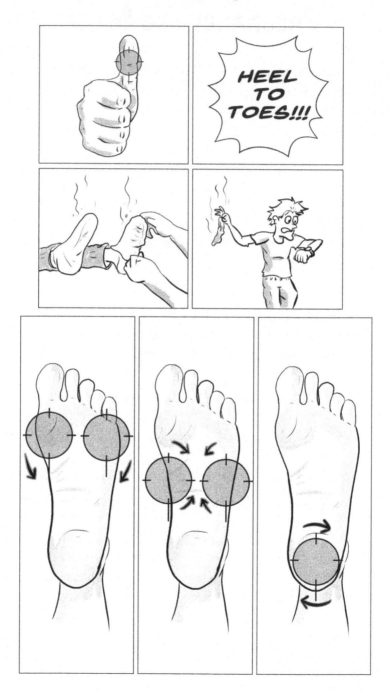

## Foot Massage

**Tip 1**: Always use the base of your thumb for the most pressure. Right where your thumb's first knuckle is.

**Tip 2**: It is best to move from heel to toes no matter what part of the foot you are rubbing.

**Step 1**: Take off her shoes and socks

**Step 2**: Wait approximately two days for the smell to go away.

**Step 3** - The Ball: Begin the massage by rubbing the bottoms of your thumbs against the ball of her feet. Work your thumbs gently toward her toes. Pull toward you with your fingers on the front/top of her foot.

**Step 4** - The Arch: Using the base of your thumb, gently move to rubbing the inside of her arch. This will feel really good but if you push too hard it will hurt her.

**Step 5** - The Heel: The best way to massage the heel that I have found is to squeeze it between your palm and fingers. Think of gripping a baseball right in the palm of your hand. Some twisting might feel nice too. The heel is challenging so, do your best. Massage the heel when you need to give the ball and the arch of the foot a break.

# Photos, Videos, & Memorabilia

Pregnancy is a wild ride, especially if this is your first experience. If your first child is the first grandchild as well, expect the flurry of activity to reach near hurricane status. Everyone I talk to about pregnancy and raising children advises me to take pictures.

With technology moving as fast as possible, documenting your journey is easier than ever before. Unless you or your wife are photographers, don't feel the need to purchase a new fancy digital camera. Your cell phone can probably do everything you will want.

I wondered, at first, what I should capture with pictures and video. Looking back, I advise you to just document everything. If you have the thought, "Maybe I should take a picture," just do it, big guy. You can take the time to go through your photos and delete the bad stuff another time—but, you won't, and it's okay. When your wife tells you it's too much, then you can start to dial back.

Right now, you should be concerned with capturing the special moments. Your wife will thank you later when she wants a photo book, or an edited home movie, of the whole nine-month experience.

I have only one disclaimer on this topic. Don't get so caught up in documenting the moment that you actually miss out. A photo right after you see the positive pregnancy test is better than a video of your wife taking the test.

If you want to plan to capture a specific moment, you'll need another person doing the camera work. Later, in the third trimester we will revisit this topic. For now, just take pictures and record video.

# ENERGY

A woman's energy levels are a funny business. Changes in her energy stem from her emotions, and emotions can change on a whim. After a few weeks of constant nausea, and being almost home-bound by fatigue, you should expect some pent-up energy.

If your wife wants to suddenly plug back into the world, your job is to help her do that. Nights out with friends, dinner with loved ones, movies and concerts, and sporting events are all encouraged. One of your goals as the sidekick is to help your hero make memories. Those experiences don't always have to be with you, but many of them should be. You want to look back and say, "Remember when you were pregnant and we…".

My wife was pregnant during the summer months and that was the year she learned to love baseball. She was so tired of being cooped up that she was up for almost anything, as long as it was not home. A local minor league team was the perfect answer. By the fourth game of the season, my wife knew player's names, the rules, and she had a favorite snow cone flavor for each day of the week.

The point is, we were out of the house, but she could sit when she needed to. We were spending time together. We made great memories. And, as a bonus, I got to watch a lot of baseball.

# THE BUILD UP

As life events go, pregnancy is likely to rank among the most challenging.

A great sidekick knows how to make their hero feel better. Even when the situation seems bleak or insurmountable, the right words can turn things around fast.

Author Steve Goodier nailed it when he said, "Sincere compliments cost nothing and can accomplish much. In any relationship, they are the applause that refreshes."

Science has shown a persons' brain works the same way whether you give them cash or pay them a compliment.

Imagine going through pregnancy alone. Consider what an awful, lonely experience that could be. Some women will endure pregnancy alone for reasons often outside their control, but your hero shouldn't have to. The reality is, you are the sidekick— and it is up to you to make all the difference.

Her physical changes will result in sexual insecurities. She will gain weight, she may lose some hair, and her skin may break out. None of this will matter in the long run because you're there for her.

There are at least two times you must be ready with a compliment.

1. When she is feeling poorly about herself (ugly, fat, clumsy, forgetful).

2. When she has already given something the best effort she could.

You want her to feel loved and noticed for her effort. At the end of the day, she should never doubt your support. Compliments are another way to make sure your hero gets what she needs from her trusty sidekick.

# HEAD SCRATCH

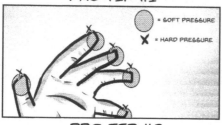

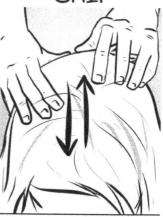

## Head Rub

My wife says there is nothing better than a good head rub, I don't agree, but this is about her, not you.

**Pro tip**: use the pads of your fingers and your nails, alternating periodically between the different kinds of pressure.

**Pro tip**: Start at the front hairline, or at the base of her neck. Don't jump around. A steady progression is important.

**Pro tip**: Moaning is an important indicator that you're doing things correctly, especially when giving head rubs. Pay attention to how she responds. If she seems to like something, keep it up!

**Step 1**: Make sure her hair is down and loose. Unless you're going for a spontaneous surprise head rub (you can sometimes earn major points that way). Have her pull out all bobby pins, hair ties, gasket rings, piston converters, and bottle openers from her hair.

**Step 2**: Use gentle pressure at first. The best technique is to ease her into the increased pressure on her head as the head rub progresses.

**Step 3**: Use the pads of your fingertips to apply pressure on your wife's scalp. Stick to three kinds of pressure. 1) Press the soft pad of your fingertip into her scalp and slowly move the skin of her scalp with your fingers. Don't let your fingers slide around at all. Be careful not to press too hard. 2) Using the pads of your fingers, massage her scalp, but loosen up the pressure enough to let your fingers slide around. 3) Use your fingernails to gently scratch her scalp.

# It's All a Gag

No, I'm not saying everything is a big joke. What I am saying is, your hero will probably gag and choke on anything within three feet of her mouth. From pickles to popsicles, donuts to dry goods, your beautiful hero is always at risk.

If you're paying attention, you can actually watch your hero attempt to avoid a full-on choking fit. Your wife will eat something and you'll see a thought flash across her face. Then she will attempt a hard swallow. Things quickly move into a grunting cough. If—or when—this string of techniques doesn't work, you'll see heavy breathing and then dry heaving. Obviously I am making light, but the truth is, many women experience a narrowing of their throat during pregnancy.

Your best sidekick move is to have something for her to drink—not alcohol. Water is always your best option. Next-level sidekicking would probably include having a hair tie in your pocket in the event of full-on vomiting.

Choking and gagging are not fun, and all we can hope to do is be ready with a hug, a tissue to wipe her mouth, and our vigilant support.

**Side Note:** These moments are not the place for your innuendo-centered jokes. Even though they will come to mind, you must resist the urge to compare anything!

## Back Scratches

1. Pressure just ask her but start with light pressure.
2. Have just enough nail. Too much is bad. Too little is bad.
3. Be willing to scratch in weird places (armpit) if she needs it, you just make it happen.
4. Take her shirt off if you can. It always feels better to her directly on her skin.

**Method 1**: Small areas. Complete before moving on.
**Method 2**: Large areas. No patterns. No method.

**Pro Tip**: If she moans, you got it.
**Pro Tip**: if she leans into the scratching, also a great sign. Stay there longer.

# Back Scratches

# Mopping the Floor

## Floor Mopping

Too many people make mopping the floor harder than it needs to be. Here are the most simple instructions ever. Sweeping is like brushing. Mopping is like scrubbing.

**Tools**:
- Dust Pan & Broom
- Mop
- Bucket of Water
- Cleaning Solution
- Clean Socks
- A Plan

**Pro Tip 1**: Wear clean socks while you mop. This will help you avoid leaving oily or dirty footprints all over the floor you should have just cleaned.

**Pro Tip 2**: Plan your escape. Start in a corner, at the back of the room. Mop backward toward your exit. You don't want to have to walk over the floor you just mopped to get out of the corner you worked yourself into. The floor will not be fully cleaned until the moisture has dried.

**Step 1**: Sweep the floor really well. If you pick up the surface-level dirt, your mop can focus on the stuff stuck to the floor. This is the goal. Put all of the dirt you swept into a dustpan and get it out of the way into the trash/outside.

Step 2: Fill a bucket with warm water. It doesn't need to be super hot but warm water is always best. You need to put the cleaning solution in with the warm water.

**Step 3**: Wet your mop. You don't want the mop soaking wet. Mopping does not include sloshing water all over the floor.

**Step 4**: With your wet mop, sweep the floor...basically. You handle the mop in the same way you would handle a broom, but you want to push hard in order to scrub the gunk from the floor.

**Step 5**: After you scrub a section of the floor three or four times, stick the mop back in the bucket. Rinse the gunk off the mop and fill it up with clean (ish) water and more cleaner. Repeat this process until the floor is scrubbed clean.

# SUCK IT UP, BUTTERCUP

Everywhere you go, someone will comment on how beautiful pregnant women are. This message is so common, you may find yourself repeating it just because it is the right thing to say. Let me set the record straight. Pregnant women you don't live with, like the ones on TV, might possess some unidentifiable radiance. Pregnant women in the real world, like the one you live with, are sort of...gross.

What nobody tells you about are the times when a pregnant woman will wear the same sweatpants for three days straight. She hasn't left the house—even to get the mail—in a week. While pregnancy facilitates the miracle of life, the true miracle during pregnancy is the one time your wife makes an effort to be presentable and actually leaves the house.

People who say your wife looks great when you leave the house are praising her for the temporary break from the bed and her favorite stretchy pants.

I won't go into all of the potential nastiness you could see. What I will say is, a pregnant woman's body is changing. Much of what happens is out of their control and they are always uncomfortable. You will see, smell, hear, and clean a bit of everything.

As a sidekick, your job is simple.

1.  Tease her only if it will make her laugh.

2.  Keep your true feelings buried, unless things get out of control. You'll know when.

3.  Praise her for her efforts, especially cleaning up and going out in public because it takes a lot of work.

# SYMPATHY WEIGHT

Did you actually skip ahead to read this first? Bravo, you done good.

In every great sidekick–hero relationship, there comes a point when the sidekick offers to sacrifice their life for the hero. Fortunately, these acts of selfless valor rarely end in the sidekick's death. The important thing is the physical sacrifice offered.

Sympathy weight is nearly inevitable. Only the most ardent and disciplined will escape the pending doom. You know it's coming, the way Samwise Gamgee knew he and Frodo might die on their way to Mordor. Consider your weight gain a noble result of the harsh journey. A battle scar, which will absolutely live on in every photograph.

**DISCLAIMER:** Just because you know it's coming, does not give you permission to eat like a wild boar in the jungles of Borneo. Becoming sick, or lacking the strength to get your wife to the hospital, will make you a burden rather than a support. After your hero gives birth, she will need to begin cutting her pregnancy weight. You will need to support that effort as well. So, remember, every pound you pack on will need to be worked off. All I am saying is, don't let things get out of control.

Set personal limits. Follow an exercise routine that helps you perform your tasks as a sidekick. But, in the end, don't be too hard on yourself when your journey leaves its scar.

# Continue Doing
# Important Things

A nswer the following questions:

What activities do you value the most?

What are your favorite things to do with your wife?

What traditions do you want to continue once you have a child?

Make a list of the most important activities in your life. Use the questions you just read as a guide, but I suggest you actually write down your answers. Pregnancy will make those activities harder to do—the first trimester proved that. Each activity requires time, effort, and some preparation. You have to commit to making time for the most important activities during pregnancy. If you don't, you will risk losing them forever.

My list included: making time for writing, attending a weekly church service, and eating home-cooked meals regularly. Let's use going to church to illustrate what I mean.

First, going to church requires going outside, during the day, which my beloved hero did not love to do. All of her church-appropriate clothes didn't fit her (neither did mine, see the previous chapter on sympathy weight). Our congregation met during lunchtime and my wife was hungry. Also, since church happened on the weekends, we were both tired from our week of work, school, and pregnancy. See what I mean? Attending church was important, but during pregnancy the meeting was super hard to deal with.

If we kept skipping church during pregnancy, we would have never attended church when there was a third—way more challenging—person to worry about. If you don't keep doing the things that are important to you, it may take you months to get back into those habits.

Maybe going to the gym is your thing. Maybe you don't want to skip poker night with your buddies. Whether it includes your wife, or not, if it's important to you, keep doing it. Mark your territory and stick to it.

Here are a few things to keep in mind:

1. Make sure your list is not too long. I suggest picking two to three items maximum. This is not an excuse for you to be selfish, but you do need to take care of yourself.

2. Encourage your wife to do this with you. She should have her own list. She needs to keep up with her friendships and maintain her goals as well.

3. Communicate your needs and listen to your wife's needs. Be honest with each other about things that are truly important.

Prepare to be flexible. You're still the sidekick, and if you get the emergency call, your poker night is not as important as the hero who needs you.

# FOOD FOR THOUGHT

This chapter covers random things that just don't fit in anywhere else. But, they are important anyway.

**SUNSCREEN:** Your pregnant hero can use sunscreen. The predominant belief is that if it's safe for the baby, it's safe during pregnancy. SPF 30 to SPF 50 is recommended. Use a sunblock without micro-particles that might be absorbed into the skin. Apply no less than every two hours.

**WATER WARS:** This is absolutely an invitation to start water fights with your wife. She's probably slower than you, and her warped center of gravity will skew her accuracy. Realistically, dehydration can harm your hero and the baby. Your job will be to make sure everyone has a great time wherever you go. Do this by helping your hero get enough water, even if that means a full-blown super soaker attack.

The typical person needs around one half to one whole gallon of water each day. Athletes require a gallon, and growing a human is nothing short of an Olympic event.

**FEET:** If the hero of your story is into the second trimester, it's a fair bet she is carrying more weight than she ever has. Even special forces guys get to drop their gear now and then. Your hero is carrying excess weight for about twenty weeks...all day. Her feet will begin to trouble her almost as often as her bladder will.

Unless either of you has a foot phobia, try massaging her feet periodically. This gives you quality time and helps to alleviate her pain. Consider a simple pair of gel-cushioned shoe inserts. This is way cheaper than a custom orthotic, or that really "comfortable" pair of Gucci sandals she's had her eye on.

Be prepared for your hero to outgrow her shoes. Yes, her feet will likely swell. She may never fit into her pre-pregnancy shoes ever again.

**HAVE FUN:** Don't let pregnancy stop you from getting the most out of your life. Plan activities, schedule and attend events, and soak up as much Vitamin D as you can. It's good for the baby's development and it's essential for your wife's mental health.

# Laundry Guide

## Laundry

You can't just put everything in the same load. Whites can only be washed with whites. If it's dark, it must be washed with darks. If it's red, at all, it goes with darks. Towels are too abrasive to be washed with anything else.

1. Separate the clothing
2. Washing machine should only be about ½ full for the best wash results
3. Colors and Darks washed on warm. Whites always washed on hot.
4. Do NOT leave it in the washing machine. You'll have a mildew problem fast
5. Transfer clothes to the dryer as quickly as possible once the wash cycle is complete.
6. Avoid fabric softeners during pregnancy because your wife already has sensitive skin

# THE WIFE BITE

It's Saturday afternoon and your stomach sends a message to your brain. It's time to eat. You walk into the kitchen, inventory your options, and you decide to make a sandwich. Because you are an all-star sidekick, you ask your wife if she would like a sandwich too. She says no. So, you lovingly prepare your sandwich. Again, because you are already in the swing of things, you put away the ingredients and clean up before you eat.

Without fail, the moment you sit down, your wife will ask for some of your sandwich. My wife always says she wants "just one bite," but in the end, that's a big fat lie. I know what you're thinking. She should have said yes when you asked her if she wanted you to make her something. She had her chance! Whether you give up the one you just made, or make her another, you have to dig out every ingredient and do it all over again. Either way, you're making another sandwich.

There is only one way to proactively solve this problem without losing your cool: the Wife Bite. When you decide to make yourself a sandwich—or anything else—ask your wife if she would like a sandwich. If she says no, save yourself the trouble by preparing a second sandwich. It could be the same size as the one you make for yourself, or it can be a smaller portion. Either way, make two. When your wife changes her mind, you're already covered. If, somehow, she never asks you to share, you have another sandwich prepared for later.

Win the battle by preparing in advance and score points for being thoughtful. Always prep a wife bite.

# The Body Pillow

# THE REPEATER

Similar to the wife bite, the repeater will save you time and help you avoid possible problems. Here's the situation.

You think to yourself, a burger sounds great right about now.

## DON'T PUT THIS BOOK DOWN TO GET
## A BURGER UNTIL YOU READ THIS

Before you even start preparing to leave, ask your wife if she would like something from whichever burger joint you've chosen. If she says no, that is when you start getting ready to leave. Take your time packing up.

Casually put on your shoes. Slowly pick up your wallet. Mosey over to pick up the keys. As you are about to leave ask your wife the same question, but in a different way. Between the first time you asked the question and the second time, your hero has been thinking about burgers—or whatever she likes from the place you said you're going. Giving her a second chance will magically connect the dots in her pregnancy brain. She'll say, "Oh, I don't know, maybe a..." followed by a meal request.

You get to do something nice for your wife. You get to take a break from your surroundings. You avoid having to go back out—or sharing three-quarters of your meal—once the smell of french fries rattles your wife's brain.

During the second trimester, she will likely feel great and want to go with you. I included it in the second trimester because you should have this practiced and perfected by the time you enter the third trimester. By then she will be so uncomfortable she won't want to move, and you'll be handling most of the food.

# THE KICKOFF

Trust is a big part of what makes a great hero-sidekick relationship. When the hero explains something only they understand, the sidekick's faith carries the relationship along. Sherlock Holmes is a perfect example.

When the mystery begins to reveal itself in Holmes' brain, he prattles on, mumbling unintelligible streams of thought. Dr. Watson tries to follow along before simply waiting for Holmes to summarize. Like Holmes, your hero needs a sounding board. At the least she needs someone else in the room for when she starts to feel crazy. The first time your wife feels the baby kick, act like Watson.

Your wife is going to wonder whether the baby is kicking or if that last taco just didn't agree with her. In no time, she will begin to make a clear distinction between incoming flatulence and the baby moving around. She will grab your hand, press your palm to her belly, and she'll look as though she is straining to hear something. You'll look into her eyes, wondering if something is supposed to happen. You'll feel nothing and begin to worry about her plans to pass gas at that exact moment.

Somewhere between the first and the seven-thousandth time this happens, the baby will kick, and you'll actually feel it. Then you'll know, for sure, she's not crazy.

Like Dr. Watson, a good sidekick hangs in there, trying to see the logic and, eventually, validating the hero. Yes, the ultrasound showed you there was a baby. But actually feeling the baby move will take reality to a new level for your hero. She will be more excited than when Sherlock Holmes cracks a case. It's the first physical sign that her pain and discomfort have not been in vain.

I didn't feel our daughter kick until the third trimester. I didn't understand why my wife was so excited. I still don't. Remember that scene from *Alien* …? That's what a kicking baby makes me think of. If you haven't seen the film, don't. If you have, I'm not sorry I brought it up. Misery loves company.

# Mood Swings
# & More Communication

The second trimester will have your hero in a near constant state of hormone imbalance. My wife experienced immense joy, heartbreaking sadness, wild fits of laughter, and unparalleled apathy during a taco commercial on TV.

There is no method to the madness. There is no silver-bullet solution. All you can do is be resilient when things get hard. Be grateful when things are pleasant. No matter what, be loving and understanding. All relationships should have established boundaries, and pregnancy is not a permission slip for her to run all over you and let her emotions rule the entire kingdom.

As her trusty sidekick, you are the one she should feel most comfortable with. She needs to be reminded that you are not going anywhere and that you'll be there for her. The key to having that conversation is to mean what you say.

You may be thinking, "if she doesn't know I'm sticking around after what I put up with during the first trimester..." Remember, pregnancy brain is real, and that's why she needs lots of reminders that you're not going anywhere. Just like she needs help remembering that baking soda and powdered sugar are not the same thing, no matter what they look like.

# Lifting Heavy Things

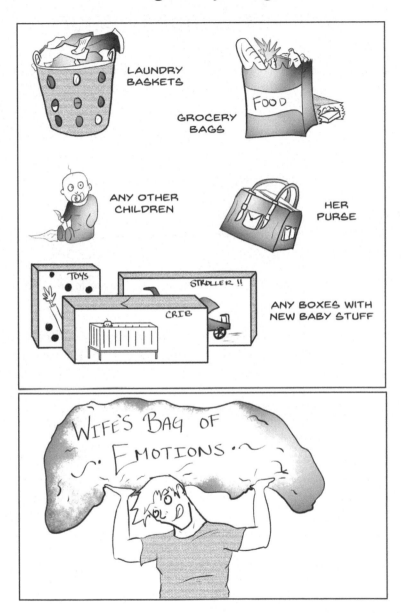

# ANOTHER LIBIDO CHANGE

Most men report their wives' have an increased sexual appetite during phase two of the journey. Some men even say they have a hard time keeping up with their wife's new-found sexual hunger. This sounds like a bad joke or too good to be true, right? Here's the scoop.

1. After the sickness and fatigue of trimester one, she has more energy.

2. Breast sensitivity increases. For some women, this results in too much sensitivity. For others, it makes everything better.

3. Her body produces mass amounts of hormones promoting affection and intimacy.

4. She experiences increased blood flow and improved circulation. That means there will be an increased level of sensitivity in the bat cave.

All of this combines to increase your hero's ability to experience more pleasurable and more frequent orgasms.

Because you're new to this, as I was, you may be wanting answers about how sex works in the second trimester. Does sex hurt the baby? The answer is no, and no, it doesn't matter how well endowed you are.

Just like everything else, communication is central to success. Talk with your hero and set boundaries if you need to. Find out what her boundaries are. Keep in mind you'll need to continually re-evaluate the boundaries as her body changes.

Whether your wife won't leave you alone, or if sex never crosses her mind, keep talking about it. You both have needs and you both deserve to have those needs respected.

# GENDER REVEAL

Despite the fifty-fifty odds, the tension can run pretty high as people discuss whether your baby will be a boy or a girl. Like a king, you may hope your first child is a boy, fulfilling your desire to produce an heir to the throne. On the other hand, you may have always felt that all of your children will be girls. No matter what, people will discuss the gender of your future child.

When the time comes to discover the gender for yourself, you have two options. Either you learn the baby's gender before they are born, or you wait to see for yourself. Either decision is fine, but discovering the gender early does have amusing benefits because how you decide to tell the world is the fun part.

You may choose to keep it low-key by sending a letter or an email. Even a phone call works. Staging a creative photo is fun, and social media is filled with unique ideas. At the end of the day, however, I prefer the party. Having another chance to celebrate and feel the love from your people is always justifiable. Whether you take care of the party preparations yourself or ask for help, it doesn't matter. Basically, all you need to worry about is making sure people know when and where to show up. After that, focus on the delivery method.

Finding a fun way to use color—either pink or blue—is the most common approach. To keep things simple, I'll stick to those here. My wife and I bought a bunch of silly string and wrapped the cans in black paper. We gave our guests a can each and, after a countdown, they sprayed us with pink silly string.

My sister and her husband didn't want to learn the gender of their baby until everyone else did. To pull this off, they asked me to be the only person who knew and to keep the information top secret. I cut open a hollow training baseball, filled it with colored powder, loosely sealed the ball, and brought it to the party. My sister pitched the baseball to her husband. He took a swing at the ball and it exploded in a cloud of blue powder.

Revealing the gender should be enjoyable. Bringing more celebration to the journey, and reminding your hero that she is supported by those she loves, is always a good decision. Memories will be created and those are worth their weight in gold.

# Stabilizing a Pregnant Woman

# Belly Butter Jelly Time

As the bump begins to grow, your hero is at risk. The risk is nothing more than a side effect of pregnancy, but it is not worth ignoring. I'm talking about stretch marks. I say this is a risk because your hero's future self-image may be affected. Luckily, there is something you can do about it—belly butter.

There are a million companies producing their own version of the same basic product. A combination of Vitamin E and moisturizer aimed at preventing stretch marks. Pick one that smells good, isn't too oily, and use it daily.

Depending on how your wife gains weight, you will want to encourage treating more than just her belly. Her inner thighs, love handles, under-arms, and breasts may be affected. Demonstrate your sensitivity and unfailing support with two easy steps.

1. Buy some cream

2. Say something like, "I hear this is awesome stuff. Let me help you put it on."

You win points for thoughtfulness now and in the future.

# BROWSING FOR BABY

Your wife—and you too, big guy—will want to go "look at cute baby stuff." This is an acceptable activity. It will get you both out of the house, and you'll begin to see how expensive the "cute" baby stuff is. That's why we are talking about browsing.

Unless you can withstand the urge to buy everything, you should go in with a gameplan. You and your wife will want to buy at least one or two things. Do whatever you think is best, but I recommend limiting your spending on clothing and cute shoes. Save your money until after the baby shower—or showers. We will talk about that during the third trimester.

Babies don't need much and, since we're being honest, I don't know many parents who change their baby's clothes every single day. If you must buy an article of clothing, I suggest you buy that awesome onesie with your team's logo on it. Nobody but you will ever buy it for your baby, so you can feel secure with that purchase.

If you really must spend money on your baby, buy diapers. Seriously, it's been this long and you still haven't started buying diapers, have you?

# INTRODUCTION
## TO THE THIRD TRIMESTER

The third trimester is a bit like preparing to live off the grid. You know the end is coming and you don't want to be unprepared. We have to get you ready to handle baby showers, diaper bags, and your wife's center of gravity. We also need to talk about sex. And, yes, it changes again. The third trimester is divided into three parts.

**Part I** covers the rest of the pregnancy process.

**Part II** is about preparing for the hospital and the birth.

**Part III** is all about preparing for your new roommate.

Unless you prefer to wallow in the turmoil of uncertainty, keeping yourself busy is the only way to survive.

Life, at this point, feels like trying to run under water. It's going to feel like losing three years of your life. Generally, the final phase of pregnancy is the most difficult for the soon-to-be father. The challenge is mostly in your mind—so you've got that going for you. By now, you should be used to occasional cravings and sudden mood swings. Each day brings new excitement and new anxiety and the slow burn of anticipation is not easy.

Everywhere you go, someone will feel compelled to tell you not to worry. You will want to shrug those comments aside, but very soon, you will need that support. Worries will also come, and that's okay because I am going to show you some ways to apply all of that nervous energy. Luckily, there is a deadline. And you, my friend, have some practical tasks to accomplish. You are officially allowed to geek out about what size of stroller you want, which is the safest car seat, and how to customize your diaper bag.

Think of it this way: the third trimester is the final chapter in book one of your saga. When this is over, when your hero slays the dragon, you earn the title of Daddy. In that magical moment, you begin your own journey as Super Dad.

# BABY SHOWER GUIDE

A baby shower is a party, for your hero, to celebrate the soon-to-be baby in her life. Think of it as a bridal shower for her uterus. Aside from simply celebrating, baby showers are intended to help the new mother prepare. Gifts are usually given and they most often come in the form of baby clothes, cribs, swings, breast-feeding stuff, and plush toys.

Typically, these parties will be planned for the final weeks before the birth. The first rule of the baby shower is, there are no rules for baby showers. Some women have multiple showers. Her friends may throw a party. Her mom may host another. Your mother may want to offer her support with a separate event. Whether your wife has one or more than one baby shower, here is what you need to know.

When I first heard about my wife's baby showers, I added the dates to the family calendar and promptly forgot about them. I thought this was a thing women did, for women—which meant "no men aloud." Boy, did I have a lot to learn.

Most of the time, you will not be expected to attend a baby shower. That is great because it jives with your default opinion of not wanting to be there anyway. However, sometimes you will be expected to attend. Other times, you will be given the choice. Rather than agonizing over the options, here is what I recommend.

1. If you are invited, ask if other men will be at the party. You don't want to be the only man at the big giant hen party in the sky. If you will be the only man attending, hopefully your wife will realize your discomfort, and let you off the hook.

2. If the party is being hosted by someone on your side of the family—like your mother—you should plan to attend. Other hostesses may include, your sister(s), your grandmother, etc. These people want to support you as much, or more, than they

are celebrating your wife. You're going to be a dad and they want to celebrate that with you.

    a.    If your family is hosting, offer to help. Bring some treats, make a decoration, and do whatever you think will help make the party go well. I mixed virgin mojitos for three hours during the baby shower my mother hosted.

2.    If you are invited to another couple's shower it is your duty to think of the father-to-be. He wants practical stuff, like diapers; or fun stuff, like a box of ammunition. Don't bring adorable baby clothes to your buddy.

# Emotions!

Look, you're not a mind reader. I know your wife wishes you were, but you're not. However, it is important that you have some idea about how she is feeling and the thoughts driving those feelings. This is an example of your wife's thought spirals at any given time. Consider these and ask yourself how your hero must feel when she has thoughts like these.

- What if something happens to the baby during delivery?

- The baby is going to look so cute in that new onesie I bought!

- What if something happens to me during delivery?

- I can't take this back...this is happening!

- I'm so excited!

- If the baby is sick, will I always regret drinking that Diet Coke during pregnancy?

- What kind of mother will I be? Will I be like my mom? Is that good or bad?

- What kind of personality will the baby have? Will the baby be sweet or sassy?

- What if there is something wrong with the baby at birth? What if there are complications?

- Is labor going to hurt? Will I do it naturally? Do I want an epidural?

- Will the baby freak out my husband? Will he leave us? Am I going to have to do this alone?

Communication and empathy are the keys to being a sidekick during pregnancy. Your wife's thoughts are constantly rotating between joy and terror, and that is what is making her crazy.

So the next time your wife has that glassy-eyed far away stare, know that her brain is trying to kill her with these awful thought spirals. Be there if she needs to talk.

# PHYSICAL CHALLENGES

Everything you have heard about women being sore, tired, and uncomfortable during the third trimester is all true. My wife began dropping everything. Sometimes it was funny. Other times she was embarrassed. Occasionally, it was expensive. Not all women have butterfingers, but most women experience many of the following challenges.

**GRAVITY:** The excess weight makes your cute wife very wobbly. Things are especially hard when her feet and her knees begin to hurt. In the third trimester, she is nearly always a fall risk.

**SPEECH:** I don't know why, but many pregnant women seem to get tongue-tied a lot In the late stages of pregnancy. Don't laugh too much, she already feels stupid.

**GAS:** The baby takes up a lot of room by this point. If your wife is gassy at all, it's going to be impossible for her to be discreet about it, if she even knows it's coming. Many women find out they farted at the same time you find out. She says she's sorry, but she's not. Either she truly can't help it, or it just feels too good to relieve a bit of the pressure. This is not an invitation for you to compete. Don't be like that.

**PEE:** Let's just get this out of the way now. She needs to urinate every 45.3 seconds for the same reasons she can't hold her gas. There is nothing she can do about it and you just have to be patient.

**SWELLING:** A big reason your wife is in so much pain all of the time is because she is swollen everywhere. It's obvious to you that her breasts are swelling, but so are her feet, her fingers, her arms, and her legs. Her skin feels like it's being stretched to its limits and that hurts.

**BREATHING:** The baby, by now, is warming up to enter the world inside your wife's belly. The kid is basically stretching, doing calisthenics, and running wind sprints before their profession-al debut. All of that is great for the baby's development but the pushing, kicking, and stretching makes it hard for your hero to breath.

With all of that making your hero uncomfortable, she will change positions frequently. She will lie down, then stand, then sit, then pace back and forth before lying back down. This is also happening at night. That's why she can't sleep well.

As the sidekick, all you can do is offer assistance, distract her when you can, and let her know it will be over soon and that everything will be worth it.

# GROOMING

The third trimester is hazardous to your wife's grooming standards. If your wife likes to keep her hero costume neat and tidy, she will be suspending her maintenance schedule in phase three. In this case, her hormones are the enemy. Her hair will grow faster and more fully. Her skin will produce way more oil. And she will sweat, a lot, for no reason.

As her sidekick, your job is to go with the flow. Anything and everything below the bump will be long forgotten. Yes, that includes the bat cave. If a razor is required, and if your sweet hero tries to fix things, it will end in disaster. Blindly, your wife cannot help but cut herself. If she does that, your ever dwindling sex life could take an inconvenient break.

Next, some women's skin actually improves and they look like a well-oiled Greek goddess. Everyone else hates them because most women have the opposite reaction. Your hero's skin may become the new enemy as pimples spring out of nowhere and she begins to resemble the junior high school version of herself. Besides turning a blind eye, you have some options for a more noble approach.

Offer to wash places which may be hard for her to reach. Or, you could buy a long-handled brush if that's more comfortable for either of you. When she asks for help, you help. If she brings up her grooming failures, or if she apologizes to you, give her a hug. Tell her she's beautiful and reassure her that it won't be that way forever. Tell her you love her just the way she is, and mean it.

Lastly, encourage her to look nice and give her ample time to make herself as presentable as she wants to be. There will be times when she will want to look great. Somewhere during the process, things will get too hard, and she will want to throw up her hands in surrender. She will put on her week-old sweatpants and refuse to leave the house. You can gently encourage her to continue, and offer to braid her hair. She'll laugh and say you're sweet.

If she still doesn't want to get ready and look nice, find a pair of sweatpants for yourself. Nobody else matters as much as your hero. If she wants to go to a wedding reception in sweats, she can. It would be way more fun—and supportive—if you were in sweats too.

One more thing, I recommend that you try to get your hero a salon visit before she goes into labor. Plan it for a few weeks in advance of the due date. Get her a manicure, a pedicure, her hair styled, her eyelashes and eyebrows done...the whole shebang. Do whatever you think you can afford. All of this will help her feel presentable at the hospital. Not all women want this, and if your baby comes early you may not get this chance. But it's a nice gesture and if your hero feels good about it, nobody loses.

## Toe Nail Painting

1. Ask your wife what color of nail polish she would like to use
2. Clean off the toenails. Use rubbing alcohol unless someone already painted the toenails, in that case, use nail polish remover.
3. Separate your wife's toes. Roll up tissue paper, or if your wife already has toe separators, use those.
4. Apply a base coat on the toenails. It's a clear liquid looking thing that helps protect the nails from staining when using darker colors.
5. Get out the nail polish bottle and remove most of the polish from the brush. Leave a very small amount on the brush to work with. Too much is BAD.
6. **BIG TOES** - leave a bit of a gap between your brush and the skin (cuticle) lay the brush down, push the brush toward the skin, but don't let the brush touch the skin, and then pull the polish back over the nail away from the skin.
7. **SMALLER TOES** - use a dabbing method to almost dot the nail. They're so small, you won't be "brushing" paint on.
8. Apply a top coat. This makes the polish last longer. It also protects the nail.
9. Remove the toe separators. It should take 10-15 mins for the polish to dry

**Pro Tip**: Any design options, more than just the color of polish, always go on the big toe.

**Pro Tip**: Don't tell your wife you read up on how to do this. Offer to do it and either wow her with your knowledge or let her guide you through the process.

# Toe Nail Painting

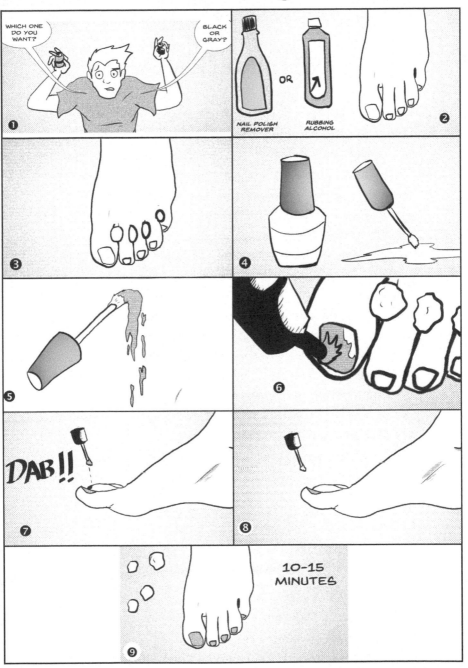

# SEX
# IN THE THIRD TRIMESTER

Sex is permitted, even into the third trimester. Again, size doesn't matter. The biggest thing to worry about are her doctor's restrictions, like whether your wife has a tear in her lady parts. There are many reasons the doctor may ask you to postpone having sexual intercourse in the third trimester, you just have to ask. If sex is okay, or if you want to work around the more traditional definition of sex, I've got you covered.

At this point, missionary position is out for two reasons. One, you don't want to break a bone in your wife's back or her pelvis. All of that pressure makes this possible. Second, being on her back will dramatically restrict blood flow to her heart and then to the baby. Cowgirl, side-by-side, or doggy-style are better options.

Because each pregnancy is so different, navigating your own sexual intimacy could be a challenge. Some couples are able to continue intercourse well into the third trimester. Other couples have to stop intercourse early in the pregnancy for medical reasons. No matter what, there will come a time when traditional intercourse is not an option, regardless of the position changes. When this happens, your sexual relationship does not need to end. There are still some great ways to keep that spark alive until the baby comes.

1. **Oral Sex:** She can give you oral sex all she wants. And, unless you have an STD, she can swallow. Providing your wife with oral pleasure should be avoided.

2. **Sex Toys For Her:** Penetration is not always the reason sex needs to stop. Ask your doctor if penetration is the reason they recommend no longer having sex. If the doc says penetration itself is not the problem, help your wife pick out a dildo. They

are a great way to avoid putting pressure on your wife and you can work different angles as your wife directs. If penetration is an issue, vibrators can provide enough stimulation to get the job done. Pleasuring your hero after a long day of "saving the world" is a great sidekick move.

3.  **Sex Toys For You:** Masturbators can provide men with a ready solution to the "no sex" problem. Talk with your wife about your needs. Ask her to be involved in the sexual experience. As with all toys, they are way more enjoyable shared than they are by yourself.

Remember to start talking about these things as early as possible. You don't need any new levels of discomfort creating barriers while everything is already upside down. After your wife gives birth, there is a pretty standard 4-6 week no sex rule, so have this conversation before that happens.

# ARE WE THERE YET?

The single hardest part of the third trimester is the waiting game. Somehow, time slows down. You will get to the point where you'll wake up every day asking yourself, "is today the day?" If you were ever going to start a mindfulness meditation practice, now would be the time.

When it comes down to it, your only option as the sidekick is to become a master of distraction. Your hero needs to take her mind off of all her crazy emotional thoughts. These distractions can be simple, fun activities or they can be goal-oriented and practical.

Planning activities you can do with your hero is always a good option. Remember, quality time is critical. Also, planning things you and your hero can do separately is important.

In my opinion, the best thing you can do is go out on dates. Spend time alone with each other and do things away from home. The truth is, once you have a baby, there will always be a third wheel. Unless you pay someone for a few hours of alone time, you may never be alone together again. Because your wife is pregnant, you can get away with some fun stuff. Here are some fun date ideas.

1. Go see a comedy and laugh as loudly as you want

2. Attend a sporting event and heckle the officials before you have to set an example as a parent

3. Eat at a fancy restaurant before they will dismiss you for wearing your post-pregnancy uniform—sweatpants

4. Get a couple's massage and see who can enjoy the massage louder

5. Cook a meal together and dance to your favorite tunes

Even though your hero is uncomfortable, unstable, and unable to control her gas, make the most of the time you have left. Deciding to go out on dates is a win-win situation for both of you.

# PART II:
## THE SIX-WEEK DEADLINE

Birth: the final struggle. The last challenge in your role as sidekick. Everything you have done, all of your hard work, will pay off in one climactic event. Samwise carried Frodo to the top of Mordor. Lucius Fox flooded the nuclear reactor chamber beneath Gotham City. You get your wife to a doctor, hold her hand, and know you have tied up the loose ends.

You're a killer sidekick and you've done everything you could to make pregnancy easier on your hero. From now on, this section will cover everything you can do to prepare for the hospital.

Once your wife begins having regular and frequent contractions, the sidekick's place is side-by-side with the hero. Set a goal to be prepared six-weeks before your baby's official due date.

A full-term pregnancy lasts between 39 and 40 weeks. By week 35, all of the baby's development has taken place and from then on the baby just gains weight. That means your wife could give birth to a perfectly healthy baby at 35 weeks—and it's not uncommon. This is why I have created the six-week deadline. If you can have everything done by week 34, you'll be set no matter what happens.

You're already thinking about all of the things you want to get done before the baby arrives. Now, imagine being unprepared a month early. The last thing you want is to be on your way to the hospital without a car seat, a crib, or even a diaper bag. Following the six-week deadline will help you focus and limit your worries.

# THE "GO BAG"

This is your bug-out-bag. I strongly recommend you have a bag full of essentials that you can grab at a moment's notice. Keep the bag by the front door or in the car. When the time comes to leave for the hospital, you have everything you will need in one central location.

Putting together a go bag is not easy. You might end up staying at the hospital for one or two days, or an entire week. Because you're a hot-shot at this point, you are wondering what things are essential. But you are also wondering what things would be overkill. Too much is just as bad as not enough. Don't pack more than one bag. Having a baby is kind of like Christmas; you're groggy but excited, everyone is smiling, and when you leave you'll have way more stuff than you expected.

Here is a list of crap I packed that nobody needed:

1.  Towels

2.  Breast Feeding Pillow

3.  Water Bottle

4.  Shampoo and Soap

5.  Personal Blanket and Pillow

Most maternity wards will have more than enough supplies to support even the most needy soon-to-be parents. They have pillows coming out of the woodwork and enough blankets for hurricane relief in each room.

When it comes to clothing, only worry about what your wife will wear when you leave the hospital. Your hero is going to wear her official super suit (the backless gown) from the moment she enters her room until the minute you leave. Only bring clothes that are the absolute most comfortable.

If you live close to the hospital, or if you have friends and family nearby, you don't have to pack a lot of things. You, or your people, could easily run to your place and get something you may have forgotten. If you don't live close to the hospital, or if you don't have reliable people, you might want to pack a bit more.

All you need is new underwear options, some deodorant, a toothbrush, fresh socks, and maybe a hat. You'll also need two to four fresh shirts and one extra pair of pants. Sweatpants are good because you'll likely sleep over at least one night. When you get to the hospital, leave the bag in the car. You're not checking into a hotel and you can go get anything you need from the parking lot.

| THE MASTER LIST | | | |
|---|---|---|---|
| **Hygiene** | **Makeup** | **Clothing** | **Personal** |
| Toothbrushes | Mascara | Pajama Pants for You | Laptop |
| A Razor/Shave Soap | Primer/Foundation | Underwear for Both | Book |
| Hair Ties/Bobby Pins | Eye Cream & Eye Liner | 1-3 Nursing Bras | Music Player/ Speaker |
| Hair Brush/ Comb | | Comfortable Wife Pants (like leggings) | Journal |
| Deodorant | | Comfortable Wife Shoes | Charging Cables |
| Dental Floss | | 2 Pairs of Socks (for both) | |
| | | Flip Flops (for the shower) | |

# PREPPING YOUR HERO

Believe it, or not, your hero is not as ready to have a baby as she thinks she is. Even if she puts on a strong face, there are still a lot of things you can do to prepare her for the big day.

The best thing you can do is talk to her and try to understand her fears and her hopes. Ask her what she is thinking, what she is afraid of, and how you can help. Then, don't forget to ask her about her hopes and what she is excited for.

For example, maybe she would prefer to have her own room during labor and delivery. Not every hospital offers this option. Armed with that knowledge, you can request a tour of the labor and delivery ward at the hospital. This is perfectly acceptable, and a nurse can show you what the average delivery room looks like.

You might also learn that your wife is terrified of having a c-section, or that she really doesn't want to have an epidural. Let your wife know that you will help ensure her decisions are honored during the birthing process.

Understand that people will make decisions for you if you don't already have a plan. It's up to you to communicate your plan to anyone who needs to know. By discussing her hopes and fears, you will help your hero identify what she really wants and how she truly feels. Give her peace of mind by ensuring that you will enforce her decisions while she is caught up in actually giving birth.

# PREPPING YOURSELF

L et's assume nobody else has given you a heads up on what happens in the delivery room. Before the time comes, you need to decide what sort of experience you want to have. You have three choices.

1. You can have a courtside seat and watch.

2. You can stay beside your wife and help her push.

3. You can sit out in the hall.

If the sight of blood, fecal matter, and a tiny gooey human being forced out of your wife's magic kingdom doesn't bother you, then you may want to watch.

I didn't like the idea of seeing my wife's magic kingdom bathed in blood—I wanted to continue viewing that place as the source of all that is good in this world. If this is how you feel, don't watch. Also, she would probably rather have you nearby for close support.

Another thing you should know is that the birthing process can be smelly. You may, or may not, notice that...at first.

Some men just can't handle that much stimulus, or the smell, or the sight of blood. If you know that about yourself, you may want to wait in the hallway. There is no shame in being honest with yourself, and your wife will continue to love you.

As always, talk about this stuff with your hero and come up with a plan. Don't forget to think about yourself a little bit too.

# Prepping Friends
# And Family

It is always best if you can be at the hospital with your wife. I understand this is not always possible, and if you can't be there, all is not lost.

That's why we have friends and family. If you can't be there, make sure your wife has at least one friend who can be there for her. Plan ahead if you think you'll be in this position. Ask for help.

For those of you who are able to be at the hospital, you and your hero need to talk about how public the delivery room will be. If you don't, you could have your brother, or a cousin, standing at the back of the room witnessing the miracle of life in 4K HD.

My wife and I decided we wanted all friends and family out of the delivery room during the birth. Before things got rolling, everyone was invited into the room, and my wife was showered with love and encouragement. We set up a signal for letting everyone back into the room after our daughter arrived and we got her cleaned up.

We love our friends and family. We also wanted to have one of our most important family moments to ourselves. We wanted to cherish it without too much distraction. Understand, we are fiercely independent people. Some women want their mother helping them through the thick of delivery, and I can see why.

When my mother gave birth to my brother the delivery doctor asked if a team of medical students could observe and learn. He was so premature that many of the students would likely not have another opportunity at that particular lesson until they had to deal with it themselves. My mother agreed to the request so a group of seven students witnessed the literal miracle of his birth.

It doesn't matter what you decide to do. But it does matter that you decide as a team. Inform everyone else and stick to that decision. Don't be alarmed if some people are offended that they aren't allowed in during delivery. They need to respect the decision made by you and your hero.

# Installing a Car Seat

## 2002

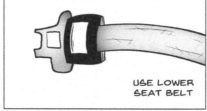

## How to Install a Car Seat

At the time of this writing, there are two methods to installing an infant car seat. Those methods are, using a seat belt and the LATCH system. Infants need to always face the rear of the vehicle, away from the windshield. When using a base, the car seat will be inserted and removed from the base with a locking mechanism.

**Vehicles made before 2002:**
If your vehicle was made after 2002, you will need to use the seat belt to secure the base of the car seat to the vehicle. All car seat bases have a seat belt path, indicated by stickers and gaps just large enough to fit a seat belt through. The lower part of the seat belt (the lap belt) is used to secure the base to the seat of the car. Feed the vehicle's seat belt through the base, lock in the seat belt buckle, and make sure the seat belt is locked. Lock the seat belt by either engaging the lock button (if your car has that) or by pulling the seat belt to its maximum length and letting the locking mechanism engage on its own. The car seat base should be held tight against the vehicle's seat. Make sure the seat belt is not twisted at any point in the installation process. The belt should be flat all the way around.

In the U.S., Vehicles Made after 2002 have the LATCH system built in: LATCH is a set of metal attachment points located between the vehicle's seat and backrest. The pair of attachment points provide a superior connection and should be used whenever possible. Purchase a car seat that supports LATCH attachment. It will come with a built vinyl belt, like a seat belt, with two hooks on either end. You attach the hooks to the attachment points. TIghten the strap.

**Installation without a base:**
You can also install a car seat without a base. Doing this will require the seat belt be guided through the belt guides, the lap belt should lie flat across the car seat, and the vehicle's seat belt should only allow 1" of movement or slack.

# What Is a C-Section?

A Cesarean section (c-section) is a surgical means of bringing baby into the world. As opposed to being forced through your hero's magical kingdom, cesarean births have the baby lifted from the womb. Many c-sections are planned but sometimes a c-section is an unexpected necessity.

Statistics show that one-in-three pregnancies require a cesarean procedure. A few factors that make c-sections more likely are:

1. If the woman is obese

2. A large baby and a small birth canal

3. If the baby is approaching the birth canal feet-first—known as breach

4. If there are multiple babies

Cesarean birth is a surgical procedure. This will extend your wife's recovery time after birth. Talk with your doctor and discuss the possibilities before your wife goes into labor. Ask the doctor about their philosophy on c-sections. Maybe that doctor is more, or less, quick to recommend the procedure than you think—or feel—is right for you.

It's important to know that there is nothing wrong with having a c-section. Your hero may believe she failed in some way but that is just not true.

Even if you plan a vaginal birth, complications during labor might make a cesarean procedure medically necessary. In some cases, it may mean saving the baby's life. Improving your understanding and having a plan save you from worrying if or when that decision needs to be made.

# WHAT ARE CONTRACTIONS
# AND HOW TO HELP

Movies and television have intensified your wife's fear of contractions basically her whole life. A woman in the third trimester spends a lot of time trying to avoid thinking about contractions because she is terrified. Despite the stereotypes, it is amazing how many different ways people explain contractions.

The doctors say it is a pregnant woman's involuntary muscle spasms responding to an innate sense that something needs to be evacuated through the Cave of Wonders...immediately. Women who have given birth will tell you contractions are when a woman's baby tries to kill her as restitution for the sins of her past.

I have no idea what a contraction feels like. What I do know is that I had to literally hold my wife up while we waited for the epidural to arrive. She couldn't sit because it hurt. She couldn't stand because she was a fall risk. I braced her under her arms as each wave of pain buckled her knees and she was incapable of doing anything but cry. It was hard to watch and to know that I couldn't do anything else to help.

Contractions are the means by which the baby is moved through the birth canal. When your wife begins pushing, you may be encouraged to hold your wife's leg up, behind the knee, as she uses your strength to leverage more abdominal pressure. If your wife has a c-section you will already be at her side to hold her hand.

You will know your wife is going into labor when she begins having contractions. The intervals between contractions are important because that is how you know when to take your wife to the hospital.

If your wife is having a strong contraction, lasting 45 to 60 seconds, every three to four minutes grab the go bag and get to the hospital. The doctor may give you different advice for measuring intervals; follow their advice over mine. Your wife's first contraction will begin as, "What the heck was that?" Eventually her response will morph until she is a moaning and screaming mess.

Remember, while you're driving to the hospital your job is to get to the big game safe and sound. Try not to be distracted by the screaming woman beside you. She needs to be sedated quickly and you need a team of nurses for support.

# What Is an Epidural?

The epidural space refers to an area of the spine made up of fat and tissue that protect the spinal cord. Within the context of pregnancy, getting "an epidural" refers to a pain management procedure where anesthesia is injected into the woman's epidural space.

Basically, a really smart doctor will insert a four-foot long needle into your hero's back.

The doctor will push a numbing pain medication through the needle and, under most circumstances, your wife's pain will be more manageable during delivery.

You might be thinking, "It blocks the nerves? Sounds like a good idea to me!" The truth is, there are at least two major reasons women question whether they should say yes or no to the procedure. The first is easily understandable—pride.

Before medical technology was as advanced as it is today, women gave birth without medicated pain management. A surprising number of women wonder if they are strong enough to give birth old school. Other women wonder whether agreeing to anesthesia makes them weak in some way. The truth is, a pregnant woman is not weak for wanting an epidural. The end.

The second reason women worry about the procedure is safety. Through the entire pregnancy women are told not to take medication. Now, suddenly it's okay to force medication into their central nervous system. It is common to have questions about how that could affect the baby. Another fear is that something will go wrong. Either it won't work at all or that the nerves may be damaged. Anesthesiologists report the chances of nerve damage are incredibly small.

In either case, you need to have a few conversations with your wife in order to understand her thoughts and feelings. I recommend having more than one discussion because the choice between meds and no meds may not be settled until that first contraction hits.

# Photography in the Delivery Room

Documenting the experience of your first child's birth is nothing new. What is new is that you need to decide how, or if, you want it documented.

Before we go any further, you should know that filming the process is not a great idea. Leave "The Miracle of Life" to PBS and that creepy 1980's health education class. That pretty much limits your options to photography.

Around 2012 people began hiring professional photographers to be in the delivery room at the climax of your hero's journey. There are two main benefits to having a photographer in the delivery room.

1. The pictures will give you insights into moments you will certainly forget.
2. Nobody misses anything or fails to provide support because they are busy trying to capture the scene.

You can direct the photographer to either capture the entire process, including the doctor's perspective, or to get everything except that particular angle. We had a photographer during our birth story and even I enjoy remembering the sleepless night, the strength of my wife, and the support I was there to give her.

A lot of men find this a strange proposal. But, consider your role in the delivery room. You are there to provide any support your hero needs: you don't have time to take pictures as well. Do one thing well instead of doing two things half-way.

## Cutting the Umbilical Cord

**Pro Tip**: Wash your hands or wear gloves.
**Pro Tip**: Don't be nervous. If you don't want to cut the cord, don't worry about it.

1. Make sure the doctor has placed clamps on the umbilical cord. Placing the clamps is not your job, but it's important anyway.
2. The doctor will give you a set of medical scissors. Take those.
3. Expect more resistance than you thought. The cord is tough and you'll need to put more effort into it than most people think.
4. Cut the umbilical cord between the two clamps the doctor or nurse has set

# Cutting the Cord

# PART III:
## THE DIAPER BAG

In this chapter I'm going to give you a simple starter list of things to have in a newborn diaper bag. Obviously everyone does it differently, so be sure to make changes to meet your needs.

Different circumstances will require different items. A harsh, cold winter will require that you carry different things than a heavy summer heat.

Also, whether you are breastfeeding or formula-feeding your baby will dictate different things to carry. Be ready to plan accordingly, but use this as a guide to getting started.

### Diaper Changes
- Wet Wipes
- At least 5 diapers
- 1-2 Dry Cloths
- Changing Pad
- 2 sets of extra baby clothes
- Baby Powder
- Rash Cream

### Feeding
*If formula feeding*
- Bottle
- *Formula Container
- *Nursing Cover or Blanket
- 1-2 Burp Cloths
- *Nipple Pads & Cream

### Miscellaneous
- Pacifiers
- Toy
- Fresh shirt for you
- Emergency Contacts Card
- Teething Chew

- Phone
- Wallet
- Keys
- Book/eReader

Don't forget to pack stuff for you too. A fresh shirt is incredibly helpful when your new bundle of joy decides to puke all over you. Or when their diaper begins to leak and you have a huge poop stain where you were holding them. The same thing goes for your phone, wallet, keys, and all other important items. It's a good idea to find a bag that will allow you to stash everything in one place.

# Changing a Diaper

## Diaper Changing

1. Put the baby on a flat, even and clean surface
2. Have the diaper rash cream on hand just in case
3. Open the wet wipes container before you get started
4. Place a fresh diaper beneath the soiled diaper
5. Undo the diaper until it is no longer wrapped around the baby
6. Hold the baby's ankles together in one hand
7. Use the front flap of the diaper to wipe the baby's bum in a large sweep downward
8. Wipe the baby's bum with a wet wipe
9. Fold the wipe and repeat wiping the baby until you either need a new wet wipe, or until the baby's bum is clean
10. Remove the soiled diaper - wrap up the used wet wipe(s) inside the soiled diaper
11. If there is a diaper rash on baby's bum, apply diaper rash cream liberally
12. Bring baby's legs down, pull the front flap of the diaper up toward baby's belly button, and use the left and right hook and loop straps to the front flap of the diaper
13. Throw away the soiled diaper

**KEY PRO TIP**: Make sure the excess ruffles lining the main part of the diaper are facing OUT!
(Ruffles Out DAD!)

# NEWBORN FIRST AID KIT

B abies are people, but they need different things when the time comes to administer first aid. Channel your inner prepper and build a baby first aid kit. You can also buy a kit. If you do, there may be things you still need or things you don't want. Either way, make sure you have one. Here is a list of the most important items for your kit.

1. **An Emergency Info Card.** Names, phone numbers for you and your wife, The doctor's info, poison control, and the nearest hospital's information.

2. **A Thermometer.** The digital thermometers are fine, but they are less accurate than an in-ear or a rectal thermometer. If you get a rectal thermometer, make sure you add water-based lube or petroleum jelly to your kit.

3. **Infant Nose Drops.** When your baby has a runny nose these will save your life.

4. **A Nasal Suction Tool.** The best on the market right now is a Nose Frida—which I recommend.

5. **Band-Aids**. Get the kind for kids. They are less sticky for baby's sensitive and tender skin.

6. **An Oral Syringe.** You will need this if you ever have to give your baby a medication, such as Benadryl, for allergic reactions. All newborn and infant medicines are liquid, so you will never go wrong having a small syringe in your kit.

7. **Hand Sanitizer.** Use this often and have other people use it before they handle your kid.

8. **Meds.** Our doctor recommended we have a motrin, acetaminophen (like Tylenol), and an antihistamine for allergies (like

Benadryl). Only give these things to your kid after consulting a doctor.

9. **A Container.** You will need something small and handy to keep all of this together. A bag or a small tupperware container work well.

In my opinion, many of the other items you will see people recommend are overkill. When baby is screaming and they can't breathe through their nose you don't have time for gloves, and you won't care.

I recommend keeping the kit in the diaper bag. Your bag and your baby will always be in the same location, so it's worth the space it will take up. Being able to administer first aid to your baby is a huge deal when you actually need it.

# THE NURSERY

There are only two feelings you can have about the baby's bedroom. Either you're excited about decorating and painting the room, or you really haven't given it much thought. Contrary to what you may think, many men get excited and involved in this particular bit of preparation.

If you are excited—about more than helping with the manual labor—embrace it wholeheartedly. If you're having a girl, selecting the perfect shade of magenta, lavender, or mint, will not put you at-risk of losing your man card. Go crazy with theme and color schemes and be as excited as you can be. For everyone else, just do whatever your hero asks you to help her with. Gently rein in her occasional unreasonable wishes.

Now, for truth time. Soon your baby's room will just be a room where the new kid sleeps...sometimes. When the baby is screaming in the middle of the night you won't remember where your face is, let alone notice the super cool baseball theme you were jazzed about.

The best way to decorate and set up the nursery is to think of you and your hero more than the baby. The kid can't even see color for almost three months. Put a rocking chair or a glider in the room. Hang framed words of encouragement and reminders about the blessings of parenthood. Make sure you have a place to change the baby and a place to put used diapers. Other important considerations are a subtle, glow-in-the-dark, three-foot tall team logo on the wall and a mini fridge in the corner.

At the end of the day, the baby needs a quiet and comfortable place to sleep. All you need is to be comfortable while you're there too.

# Swaddling a Baby

## Swaddling

This is where you get to make a baby burrito. There are no "right" ways to do this. The important thing is that you help your baby feel safe and secure by (not too) tightly wrapping them up. You can buy a pre-made swaddler, and some people love them, but I think they aren't worth the expense.

**PRO TIP**: Get a swaddle blanket that is stretchy but not a heavy material. The best ones are lightweight and breathable.

There are two ways to do this. The Triangle approach and the square approach. I think the triangle option is the better of the two.

# Putting Baby in the Car Seat

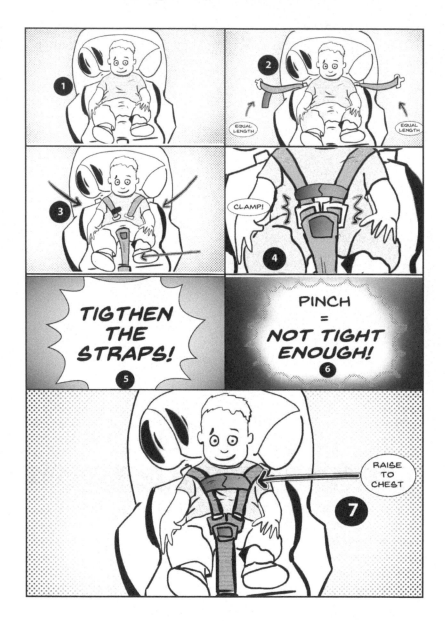

## How to Put Your Kid in the Car Seat

1. Ensure the baby's back is flush with the back of the car seats back-rest. You don't want the kid tilted to one side, or the other, but straight up and down.

2. Make sure the shoulder straps are sized properly. When putting the kid in the seat, the straps should start at, or below, the child's shoulders. There should not be a gap between where the shoulder straps start and the top of the child's shoulder.

3. The child's arms will be looped under the shoulder straps, allowing the shoulder straps to come down across the baby's chest and stomach until reaching the latch between the baby's legs.

4. Lock the left and right shoulder straps to the buckle attached to the crotch strap between the baby's legs.

5. Tighten the straps

6. Check for tightness. If you can pinch and fold the vinyl straps, it's not tight enough. Tighten until you cannot pinch and fold the shoulder straps.

7. Now, clip the sternum strap, or harness clip. It should be adjusted until it sits across the baby's chest at the armpit level.

# KITCHEN PREPARATION

Once the newly-minted bundle of screaming joy is home, your time will be spent in one of two ways. You will change diapers, feed and burp the baby, perfect your whispering skills, and change more diapers. Or, you will be preparing yourself by strategically placing diapers, wipes, and blankets anywhere you may need them. All of that work makes handling meals a bit daunting and don't even get me started on doing dishes.

1.  Plan ahead by purchasing paper or plastic cups, bowls, plates, and utensils before baby arrives. Having the ability to throw away your plate after a meal will save you time and help you avoid a pile of dirty dishes to deal with.

2.  Simplify your meal selection. Bags of microwavable pasta or stir-fry are great options. Simple sandwich ingredients are also an easy choice.

3.  Another thing you'll want to do is make everything easily reachable. If you are away while your wife is home, she needs to have the easiest possible way to feed herself.

All of this will make meals easier to deal with. The truth is, you're going to be too tired to care. If meals are too inconvenient you will go broke eating takeout two or three times per day. A stack of paper plates is worth the expense when compared to a frazzled mind and a hungry wife.

# BREASTFEEDING
# VERSUS FORMULA FEEDING

Do you and your hero want to breastfeed the baby, or are you planning on giving the kid formula? Here are some things to think about if you don't already have an answer to that question.

Many people—including the American Association of Pediatrics—recommend a child be fed breast milk exclusively for the first six months. The AAP further recommends extending that to 12 months if at all possible. Medically speaking, breast milk contains nutrients specific to your baby. Because of that, doctors report your baby being stronger and having a greater ability to fight off illness. Otherwise there are pros and cons on either side.

For example, babies who drink only breastmilk will need more frequent diaper changes. Formula fed babies digest the food slower and need fewer diaper changes. If your wife feels that her existence on earth is only good for pressing her breasts against the kid's face, she could get depressed real fast. Formula feeding means that anyone can feed the baby.

Not all women can breastfeed. Some women are able to breastfeed until suddenly they can't—this is entirely normal. Other women have medical issues that make breastfeeding impossible altogether.

Don't mistake bottle feeding for formula feeding. A woman can, and should, pump breast milk into bottles. If she is pumping and storing her milk, you can feed the baby. Your hero has been bonding with the baby for months, so now it's your turn.

By feeding with a bottle you have the chance to bond with your new little one. This is critical to the baby's development, to your relationship with the new kid, and to giving your wife much needed breaks during the day and night.

Speaking of nighttime feeding, you will also need to plan a solution for that. I recommend setting up a schedule. For example, my sister and her husband switched between days. Monday nights were his responsibility, Tuesday nights were her's, and so forth.

My wife and I took shifts. I stayed awake doing homework or working until 2:00 a.m. every day. This made it possible for my wife to get to bed by 8:00 or 9:00 p.m. She got six hours of sleep before I went to bed and her "shift" began. I woke up at 7:00 a.m. and went to school in the morning and work in the afternoon.

Bottles, whether by stored breast milk or formula, make this type of teamwork possible. By now, you'll know it's the only way to go. Make a plan and rock the plan. You've got this.

Ultimately, you have to make a decision and stick with it. Unless, of course, the decision is made for you. In that case, quit worrying about it. Formulas are just fine and I personally believe mixing breast milk and formula from time-to-time when you need to isn't going to hurt anyone.

# POSTPARTUM DEPRESSION

Even though postpartum literally means after birth, I decided to include this topic because the more preparation you can have, the better off everyone will be.

After a woman gives birth to a child, her body experiences another overhaul of her hormones. Obviously, this causes a lot of emotional turmoil. Your wife begin to realize that her body will never be the same again. She will wonder about being ready to mother a child and still maintain all of her other hopes and dreams. This is known as the "baby blues" and it could last up to two weeks. If the baby blues don't pass, your wife could be dealing with postpartum depression.

It is not uncommon for women to resent their newborn. Many women feel as though they were merely an incubator and now their role in life is to be a milk factory. For nearly a year, your hero has been the center of attention. Then the kid shows up and suddenly nobody remembers your hero is even in the same room.

Mild cases of postpartum depression can leave a new mother feeling at the end of her rope, angry, and inadequate. In severe cases, new mothers can have thoughts of harming the child or of harming themselves. After all she has been through, your hero may begin to feel that the baby would be better off without her. Or she may begin to fantasize about life without the baby. As the sidekick you must understand two things.

1.  Every single woman on earth experiences some form of postpartum depression.

2.  When she does, she is experiencing a true chemical imbalance which she has little-to-no control over.

This does not mean women are crazy. It means you have to step up your game once the baby shows up—and not just changing diapers.

Your hero needs you to look out for her, to watch her, and to help her in any way you can. Here are a few tips on how to spot postpartum depression.

- 👍 The "baby blues" didn't get better

- 👍 She mentions anything about harming herself or the baby— even a joke could indicate depression

- 👍 Sad or guilty thoughts never go away

- 👍 She loses interest in everything and simply doesn't care

- 👍 You can see it in her eyes, she's just "gone cold," uncaring, or withdrawn

- 👍 She lacks the desire to eat

Okay, so you've noticed some of those things, now what? When things get overwhelming, and the kid won't stop screaming despite her best efforts, tell her it's okay to just lie the baby down and walk away for a few minutes. She can collect herself and then go back. That is the best thing she can do when you're not also present. If you are there, both of you need to be giving each other breaks. At one point, my wife and I were switching back-and-forth every three minutes just to get a grip on our emotions.

Remind her that this is not going to last forever. Tell her stories about your baby boy growing up to play baseball and practice for the third grade spelling bee. Help her fantasize about your baby girl taking first place at the science fair and learning to ride a bike.

Get her out of the house. Go to the mall and walk around. Hit the local bookstore and try to decide which author's names are real and which are completely made up pen names. Go to a park and just lie in the grass while she soaks up the sun. Encourage her to go out with friends and have adult conversations with other people who are also pretending to hold it together.

Get a babysitter when you can or take the kid with you. Be present. Be helpful with the baby and give her breaks as often as you can. When other people want to spend time with the baby, let them, but you take care of your wife.

Even with these lifestyle changes, it is highly encouraged that she receives some kind of formal care or treatment. Maybe a short-term antidepressant would be a great idea. Maybe she needs to see a counselor for therapy. In either case, the quicker she gets help, the quicker she can go back to being the hero everyone knows and loves.

# Holding and Feeding a Baby

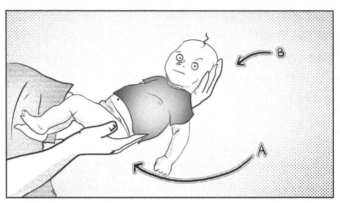

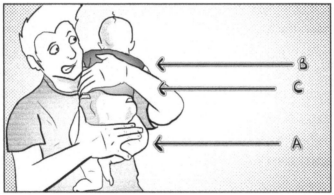

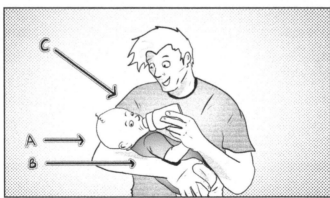

## Holding and Feeding a Baby

There are three main ways to hold a baby. At all times you must stabilize the baby's neck and head. The kid cannot hold their own head up so you have to do it for them.

1. Hold the kid in both hands
   a. Cradle the kid's bottom and hips in one hand
   b. Cradle the kid's neck and head in the palm of the other hand
2. Hold the baby on your shoulder
   a. Cradle the kid's bottom with one hand
   b. Rest the kid's chest against your shoulder
   c. Use your other hand to gently pat on the baby's back
   d. This is the position you will use to burp the baby after you feed them
3. Hold the baby like a running back holding a football
   a. Place the baby's head in the crook of your elbow
   b. Support the rest of the baby's body along the inside of your forearm
   c. Keep your arm close to your body and create a ledge for the baby to rest on between your body and your arm
   d. This is how you will feed the baby

**PRO TIP**: When feeding the baby, keep them on a 45 degree inclined angle. The baby shouldn't be parallel with the floor. The raised angle helps the baby ingest less air and helps them have fewer tummy aches, which means fewer times they'll puke all over you.

# CONCLUSION

Pregnancy is a thing of the past, and you can rest easy knowing that you did your job. You did it nobly. You handled everything the best way you could have. So, now what?

I wish I could tell you things will get easier. I wish I could tell you that you're off the hook. But, none of that is true. You may not need to rush to restock ginger ale or slather anyone in vitamin E, all of that is over, but your job description hasn't changed.

For nine months you have given yourself over to supporting a pregnant woman. Now, you will be asked to shift into a new gear as you take on a new title: The Dad.

The last thing you should do is worry. Does the workload increase a bit? Yes. Do you have to shift responsibilities, overcome new challenges, and slay new dragons? Yes. But all of these things are, to say the very least, amazing.

Here's what I suggest. Lose your sympathy weight, and help your wife lose her pregnancy weight. Become a more fully-formed team built on improved communication skills. The baby needs you to present a unified position in as many areas as possible. Establish a routine, divide responsibilities, and take charge. Lead your new family and be one with your wife as you take on life together.

One last piece of advice, go buy diapers. Seriously, why haven't you done that yet? It's the end of the book, my man.

# SIDEKICK SKILLS

## Brewing Herbal Tea

Unless you're already a tea brewing magician, you will want to avoid loose-leaf tea in a strainer. Just buy pre-made tea bags. The key here is flavor and speed.

5. Bring a pot or kettle of water until it's wicked hot (205 degrees fahrenheit). If you get really desperate you can heat a mug of water in the microwave but it's not optimal.

6. Make sure you have a clean mug

7. When the hot water is ready, place the tea bag in the hot water. (Tea in hot water is called "steeping")

8. Most herbal tea should be steeped in 205 degree water for approximately XX minutes. If you leave it in much longer than that, the tea will become bitter.

## Muscles Critical to Fatherhood

1. **Front Deltoid**: This is your shoulder, and you'll work it constantly.

2. **Biceps**: Think about all the times you'll hold the kid in the crook of your arm.

3. **Abs**: You are going to use your core more than ever.

4. **Quads**: Because you don't want to throw out your back lifting all that baby gear. Lift with your legs.

## Baking Soda Deodorizer Guide

**Step 1**: Vacuum your carpet like you've never vacuumed before. Empty the bag/canister before you start. Go slowly, be super thorough. Move stuff out of the way if you can and vacuum under everything. This step picks up all of the surface level dirt.

**Step 2**: Dump baking soda on the carpet. It will come out, don't worry. No, it won't stain or bleach your carpet. Be liberal and cover the entire carpeted area. Don't forget about stairs and carpet near bathrooms and eating areas.

**Step 3**: Walk away. You will want to let the soda sit on your carpet for several hours while the soda does it's thing.

**Step 4**: Vacuum again. Obviously you'll need to clean the soda from your carpet. Baking soda traps odor. By vacuuming the soda, you also remove the odor. Again, be thorough and go slow.

## List of Foods to Avoid

- Sushi and Most Fish
- Caffeine
- Smoking
- Alcohol
- Drugs (including most medication)
- Cured Meats (Salami & Bacon)

## Foot Massage

**Tip 1**: Always use the base of your thumb for the most pressure. Right where your thumb's first knuckle is.

**Tip 2**: It is best to move from heel to toes no matter what part of the foot you are rubbing.

**Step 1**: Take off her shoes and socks

**Step 2**: Wait approximately two days for the smell to go away.

**Step 3** - The Ball: Begin the massage by rubbing the bottoms of your thumbs against the ball of her feet. Work your thumbs gently toward her toes. Pull toward you with your fingers on the front/top of her foot.

**Step 4** - The Arch: Using the base of your thumb, gently move to rubbing the inside of her arch. This will feel really good but if you push too hard it will hurt her.

**Step 5** - The Heel: The best way to massage the heel that I have found is to squeeze it between your palm and fingers. Think of gripping a baseball right in the palm of your hand. Some twisting might feel nice too. The heel is challenging so, do your best. Massage the heel when you need to give the ball and the arch of the foot a break.

## Floor Mopping

Too many people make mopping the floor harder than it needs to be. Here are the most simple instructions ever. Sweeping is like brushing. Mopping is like scrubbing.

**Tools**:
- Dust Pan & Broom
- Mop
- Bucket of Water
- Cleaning Solution
- Clean Socks
- A Plan

**Pro Tip 1**: Wear clean socks while you mop. This will help you avoid leaving oily or dirty footprints all over the floor you should have just cleaned.

**Pro Tip 2**: Plan your escape. Start in a corner, at the back of the room. Mop backward toward your exit. You don't want to have to walk over the floor you just mopped to get out of the corner you worked yourself into. The floor will not be fully cleaned until the moisture has dried.

**Step 1**: Sweep the floor really well. If you pick up the surface-level dirt, your mop can focus on the stuff stuck to the floor. This is the goal. Put all of the dirt you swept into a dustpan and get it out of the way into the trash/outside.

Step 2: Fill a bucket with warm water. It doesn't need to be super hot but warm water is always best. You need to put the cleaning solution in with the warm water.

**Step 3**: Wet your mop. You don't want the mop soaking wet. Mopping does not include sloshing water all over the floor.

**Step 4**: With your wet mop, sweep the floor...basically. You handle the mop in the same way you would handle a broom, but you want to push hard in order to scrub the gunk from the floor.

**Step 5**: After you scrub a section of the floor three or four times, stick the mop back in the bucket. Rinse the gunk off the mop and fill it up with clean (ish) water and more cleaner. Repeat this process until the floor is scrubbed clean.

## Head Rub

My wife says there is nothing better than a good head rub, I don't agree, but this is about her, not you.

**Pro tip**: use the pads of your fingers and your nails, alternating periodically between the different kinds of pressure.
**Pro tip**: Start at the front hairline, or at the base of her neck. Don't jump around. A steady progression is important.
**Pro tip**: Moaning is an important indicator that you're doing things correctly, especially when giving head rubs. Pay attention to how she responds. If she seems to like something, keep it up!

**Step 1**: Make sure her hair is down and loose. Unless you're going for a spontaneous surprise head rub (you can sometimes earn major points that way). Have her pull out all bobby pins, hair ties, gasket rings, piston converters, and bottle openers from her hair.

**Step 2**: Use gentle pressure at first. The best technique is to ease her into the increased pressure on her head as the head rub progresses.

**Step 3**: Use the pads of your fingertips to apply pressure on your wife's scalp. Stick to three kinds of pressure. 1) Press the soft pad of your fingertip into her scalp and slowly move the skin of her scalp with your fingers. Don't let your fingers slide around at all. Be careful not to press too hard. 2) Using the pads of your fingers, massage her scalp, but loosen up the pressure enough to let your fingers slide around. 3) Use your fingernails to gently scratch her scalp.

## Back Scratches

1. Pressure just ask her but start with light pressure.
2. Have just enough nail. Too much is bad. Too little is bad.
3. Be willing to scratch in weird places (armpit) if she needs it, you just make it happen.
4. Take her shirt off if you can. It always feels better to her directly on her skin.

**Method 1**: Small areas. Complete before moving on.
**Method 2**: Large areas. No patterns. No method.

**Pro Tip**: If she moans, you got it.
**Pro Tip**: if she leans into the scratching, also a great sign. Stay there longer.

## Cleaning The Toilet

**Pro tip**: The Works is the only toilet cleaner worth a Damn.

**Tools**:
- Clorox wipes
- The Works
- Toilet bowl brush

**Step 1**: Squeeze the works inside the toilet bowl. Specifically target the upper lip inside the bowl. Let the cleaner sit while you complete steps 2 & 3.

**Step 2**: Scrub the outside of the toilet with Clorox wipes. Don't forget the outside of the bowl.

**Step 3**: clean the floor around the toilet bowl. All the way around.

**Step 4**: Scrub inside the toilet bowl with brush. Clean all surfaces, even if they are white. Hit the inside lip of the bowl pretty hard.

**Step 5**: Flush the toilet.

## Cooking For Your Wife

**Pro tip**: Do not screw this up by thinking you can cook for your wife.
**Pro tip**: Hot sauce is key. / Don't discount hot sauce.

**Step 1**: Ask your wife what kind of tacos she wants.

**Step 2**: Ask her how many tacos she wants.

**Step 3**: Get in your car and drive to the nearest taco joint. Bonus points: Drive to her favorite taco joint.

**Step 4**: DO NOT get a different kind of taco than your wife asked for.

**Step 5**: ALWAYS get more tacos than your wife asked for.

**Step 6**: Deliver tacos to your wife.

**Step 7**: Do all of this as quickly as possible.

## Cutting the Umbilical Cord

**Pro Tip**: Wash your hands or wear gloves.
**Pro Tip**: Don't be nervous. If you don't want to cut the cord, don't worry about it.

1. Make sure the doctor has placed clamps on the umbilical cord. Placing the clamps is not your job, but it's important anyway.
2. The doctor will give you a set of medical scissors. Take those.
3. Expect more resistance than you thought. The cord is tough and you'll need to put more effort into it than most people think.
4. Cut the umbilical cord between the two clamps the doctor or nurse has set

## Diaper Changing

1. Put the baby on a flat, even and clean surface
2. Have the diaper rash cream on hand just in case
3. Open the wet wipes container before you get started
4. Place a fresh diaper beneath the soiled diaper
5. Undo the diaper until it is no longer wrapped around the baby
6. Hold the baby's ankles together in one hand
7. Use the front flap of the diaper to wipe the baby's bum in a large sweep downward
8. Wipe the baby's bum with a wet wipe
9. Fold the wipe and repeat wiping the baby until you either need a new wet wipe, or until the baby's bum is clean
10. Remove the soiled diaper - wrap up the used wet wipe(s) inside the soiled diaper
11. If there is a diaper rash on baby's bum, apply diaper rash cream liberally
12. Bring baby's legs down, pull the front flap of the diaper up toward baby's belly button, and use the left and right hook and loop straps to the front flap of the diaper
13. Throw away the soiled diaper

**KEY PRO TIP**: Make sure the excess ruffles lining the main part of the diaper are facing OUT!
(Ruffles Out DAD!)

## Holding and Feeding a Baby

There are three main ways to hold a baby. At all times you must stabilize the baby's neck and head. The kid cannot hold their own head up so you have to do it for them.

1. Hold the kid in both hands
   a. Cradle the kid's bottom and hips in one hand
   b. Cradle the kid's neck and head in the palm of the other hand
2. Hold the baby on your shoulder
   a. Cradle the kid's bottom with one hand
   b. Rest the kid's chest against your shoulder
   c. Use your other hand to gently pat on the baby's back
   d. This is the position you will use to burp the baby after you feed them
3. Hold the baby like a running back holding a football
   a. Place the baby's head in the crook of your elbow
   b. Support the rest of the baby's body along the inside of your forearm
   c. Keep your arm close to your body and create a ledge for the baby to rest on between your body and your arm
   d. This is how you will feed the baby

**PRO TIP**: When feeding the baby, keep them on a 45 degree inclined angle. The baby shouldn't be parallel with the floor. The raised angle helps the baby ingest less air and helps them have fewer tummy aches, which means fewer times they'll puke all over you.

## How to Install a Car Seat

At the time of this writing, there are two methods to installing an infant car seat. Those methods are, using a seat belt and the LATCH system. Infants need to always face the rear of the vehicle, away from the windshield. When using a base, the car seat will be inserted and removed from the base with a locking mechanism.

### Vehicles made before 2002:

If your vehicle was made after 2002, you will need to use the seat belt to secure the base of the car seat to the vehicle. All car seat bases have a seat belt path, indicated by stickers and gaps just large enough to fit a seat belt through. The lower part of the seat belt (the lap belt) is used to secure the base to the seat of the car. Feed the vehicle's seat belt through the base, lock in the seat belt buckle, and make sure the seat belt is locked. Lock the seat belt by either engaging the lock button (if your car has that) or by pulling the seat belt to its maximum length and letting the locking mechanism engage on its own. The car seat base should be held tight against the vehicle's seat. Make sure the seat belt is not twisted at any point in the installation process. The belt should be flat all the way around.

In the U.S., Vehicles Made after 2002 have the LATCH system built in: LATCH is a set of metal attachment points located between the vehicle's seat and backrest. The pair of attachment points provide a superior connection and should be used whenever possible. Purchase a car seat that supports LATCH attachment. It will come with a built vinyl belt, like a seat belt, with two hooks on either end. You attach the hooks to the attachment points. Tighten the strap.

### Installation without a base:

You can also install a car seat without a base. Doing this will require the seat belt be guided through the belt guides, the lap belt should lie flat across the car seat, and the vehicle's seat belt should only allow 1" of movement or slack.

## How to Put Your Kid in the Car Seat

1. Ensure the baby's back is flush with the back of the car seats backrest. You don't want the kid tilted to one side, or the other, but straight up and down.

2. Make sure the shoulder straps are sized properly. When putting the kid in the seat, the straps should start at, or below, the child's shoulders. There should not be a gap between where the shoulder straps start and the top of the child's shoulder.

3. The child's arms will be looped under the shoulder straps, allowing the shoulder straps to come down across the baby's chest and stomach until reaching the latch between the baby's legs.

4. Lock the left and right shoulder straps to the buckle attached to the crotch strap between the baby's legs.

5. Tighten the straps

6. Check for tightness. If you can pinch and fold the vinyl straps, it's not tight enough. Tighten until you cannot pinch and fold the shoulder straps.

7. Now, clip the sternum strap, or harness clip. It should be adjusted until it sits across the baby's chest at the armpit level.

## Laundry

You can't just put everything in the same load. Whites can only be washed with whites. If it's dark, it must be washed with darks. If it's red, at all, it goes with darks. Towels are too abrasive to be washed with anything else.

1. Separate the clothing
2. Washing machine should only be about ½ full for the best wash results
3. Colors and Darks washed on warm. Whites always washed on hot.
4. Do NOT leave it in the washing machine. You'll have a mildew problem fast
5. Transfer clothes to the dryer as quickly as possible once the wash cycle is complete.
6. Avoid fabric softeners during pregnancy because your wife already has sensitive skin

## Lifting Heavy Things

**Some Common Examples to Prepare For**

1. Laundry Baskets
2. Grocery Bags
3. Any Other Children
4. Her Purse
5. Any Boxes With New Baby Stuff (Stroller, Crib, Swing, High Chair, Car Seat)
6. Draw a dude holding a box over his shoulder/on his back. The box reads "My Wife's Emotions." He is clearly struggling to keep it up.

## Swaddling

This is where you get to make a baby burrito. There are no "right" ways to do this. The important thing is that you help your baby feel safe and secure by (not too) tightly wrapping them up. You can buy a pre-made swaddler, and some people love them, but I think they aren't worth the expense.

**PRO TIP**: Get a swaddle blanket that is stretchy but not a heavy material. The best ones are lightweight and breathable.

There are two ways to do this. The Triangle approach and the square approach. I think the triangle option is the better of the two.

## Toe Nail Painting

1. Ask your wife what color of nail polish she would like to use

2. Clean off the toenails. Use rubbing alcohol unless someone already painted the toenails, in that case, use nail polish remover.

3. Separate your wife's toes. Roll up tissue paper, or if your wife already has toe separators, use those.

4. Apply a base coat on the toenails. It's a clear liquid looking thing that helps protect the nails from staining when using darker colors.

5. Get out the nail polish bottle and remove most of the polish from the brush. Leave a very small amount on the brush to work with. Too much is BAD.

6. **BIG TOES** - leave a bit of a gap between your brush and the skin (cuticle) lay the brush down, push the brush toward the skin, but don't let the brush touch the skin, and then pull the polish back over the nail away from the skin.

7. **SMALLER TOES** - use a dabbing method to almost dot the nail. They're so small, you won't be "brushing" paint on.

8. Apply a top coat. This makes the polish last longer. It also protects the nail.

9. Remove the toe separators. It should take 10-15 mins for the polish to dry

**Pro Tip**: Any design options, more than just the color of polish, always go on the big toe.

**Pro Tip**: Don't tell your wife you read up on how to do this. Offer to do it and either wow her with your knowledge or let her guide you through the process.